THE FLOURISHING STUDENT

A practical guide to promote mental fitness, well-being and resilience in Higher Education

D1270525

FABIENNE VAILES

First published in Great Britain by Practical Inspiration Publishing, 2017

Revised edition published 2022

© Fabienne Vailes, 2022
The moral rights of the author have been asserted

ISBN 9781788603331   (print)
      9781788603355   (epub)
      9781788603348   (mobi)

Every effort has been made to trace copyright holders and to obtain their permission for the use of copyright material. The publisher apologizes for any errors or omissions and would be grateful if notified of any corrections that should be incorporated in future reprints or editions of this book.

Practical Inspiration
Publishing

MIX
Paper from
responsible sources
FSC® C013604

In loving memory of my father-in-law Bernard,
who passed away on 1 September 2021.

Dedicated to my amazing, loving family and friends.

And more specifically:

To maman and papa – thank you for giving me the gift
of life. Without you both, this book wouldn't exist, and I
wouldn't be the individual I am today.

To my wonderful husband and best friend, Jason: I am
so grateful to have you by my side – always my biggest
supporter and challenger. Without your support and help,
I wouldn't have grown into the woman, wife and friend I
currently am but most importantly this book would never
have happened.

And to my fabulous boys, Thomas and Jack – I hope this
Flourishing Model (FM) serves and guides you throughout
your childhood and beyond. My wish is for you to truly
become flourishing lifelong learners.

Contents

Acknowledgements

My heartfelt thanks to:

First of all, this book would not have happened without all the prior knowledge and skills I acquired with John Seymour (of JSnlp), who taught me all that I know about NLP and in particular all the NLP techniques I have used in this book, and Adam Dacey (MindSpace), who introduced me to Mindfulness and showed me not only how to teach it but also how to introduce it into my daily life. I am forever indebted to you both!

Alison Jones, my publisher, for believing in me and in this book, and all the team at Practical Inspiration. Thanks so much for providing me with the support and platform to transform dreams into reality.

Professor Corey Keyes for allowing me to use his work and model as a base for my work and for spending some time discussing this over Skype.

Colleagues and experts (in particular, Mark Ames, Sarah Ashworth, Jeremy Christey, Ed Davis, Laurie Leitch, Amy Lewis, Knut Schroeder and Dominique Thompson) who shared their thoughts with me and agreed to give up some of their precious time to share their insights into this fascinating and important topic of mental health in Higher Education and/or to connect me with other specialists. Louise Wiles and Natalie Rothwell-Warn for sharing their knowledge and understanding of Appreciative Inquiry and its application in the field of education.

My precious friend Treesje, who every week has coached, supported and helped me reflect on some of the challenges I was experiencing.

Students and colleagues, who allowed me to use their stories to write this book. You know who you are and I am very grateful to you all!

All the amazing guests who came to speak with me on the Flourishing Education podcast as well as all the wonderful people I have met on LinkedIn since the pandemic started. To all of you: I want you to know how grateful I am for your insights and for sharing so openly with me. Our conversations have literally reshaped me (and my thinking).

You have all enabled and inspired me to create (and review) this Flourishing Model (FM).

All my colleagues and friends in the School of Modern Languages and outside university who spent some time reading this first draft and giving me feedback.

Foreword

'You are one thought away from changing your life,
if you so desire.'
p.120

On 27 February 2019 it was my University's winter Festival of Learning. As an academic with 24 years' experience, and increasingly conscious of the stresses and associated anxiety that were washing inexorably over higher education, the keynote session caught my eye: Fabienne Vailes speaking about *The Flourishing Student*. Quite simply, I will never forget that day and my first encounter with Fabienne. Shining out was her infinite and yet humble wisdom, her unfettered and authentic commitment for all young people to live healthy lives (emotionally, cognitively, physically, socially and spiritually), and her clear communication of practical ways we might achieve this. Her words and her published works have transformed me as an academic practitioner.

I absorbed the content of the first edition of *The Flourishing Student* and transferred it to my teaching and assessment to consciously embed well-being in my practice. I came to view well-being as fundamental, rather than additional, to my academic role. My students blossomed and their outcomes improved. I took Fabienne's ideas forward in my research, conceptualized as 'borderland spaces' of learning that are open to creative possibility amidst uncertainty, promoting student self-efficacy and positive mental health. I established and co-delivered a well-being workshop for

Programme Leaders across my institution and our student satisfaction scores increased. I eventually moved institution to take on a leadership role in staff development to scale up the changes I wished to make. Currently, at the University of Gloucestershire, we are adopting Fabienne's Flourishing Model and working with her directly to meet the core aim of our new Strategic Plan: to enable our students and staff to flourish and achieve their full potential.

In *The Flourishing Student* you will find a theoretically informed practical guide to promoting mental health, well-being and resilience in higher education. The book is rooted in the extensive educational, well-being, and mindfulness expertise of the author, supported by comprehensive empirical evidence in the form of hundreds of interviews and conversations with staff and students, and wide-ranging referenced literature. The chapters are eminently readable because they are undeniably warm, inviting and accessible, coupled with being lucidly organized. The book begins by illuminating the concepts of mental health, stress and well-being, and establishing the current state of student mental health in UK higher education. It highlights the benefits of flourishing and introduces a novel Flourishing Model based in a metaphor of students as flowers that are able to grow and thrive, given the right conditions, in the wider ecological system of the university. This wonderful analogy enables Fabienne to explore with ease the many factors that play a role in student growth and development by reviewing a flower's anatomy (the roots, for example, represent memories, values, beliefs and metaprograms, the stem represents mindset, and the flower head is composed of nourishing health and skills petals). Using this model, Fabienne presents a toolbox of techniques and activities to enable you to develop your own well-being and that of your students, suitable for your context. The book finishes by both inviting and challenging institutions to take a systemic approach to building communities that can foster diversity, inclusion, and resilience holistically, moving beyond competitiveness to co-operation and co-creation through Appreciative Enquiry.

Fabienne has written *The Flourishing Student* in a refreshingly unassuming style. The book will draw you in, invigorate you and provide you with the principles, skills and confidence you need to think and act more positively with respect to student well-being. It is a liberating read that can free you from your routinized perspectives about teaching and learning, instead offering you a stimulating, mindful and rewarding approach to your practice. What I particularly enjoy in the book is the many times Fabienne challenges taken-for-granted norms, such as confronting negative linguistics around mental health, re-envisioning stress as a 'friend', thereby enabling us to choose how we respond to it, and welcoming emotions in the classroom. Every one of these challenges will open your eyes to achievable opportunities for positive change.

The Flourishing Student makes infinite sense. Whether you are an academic, a professional staff member, a senior leader, or if you sit outside of higher education, I am sure you will find this book inspiring and productive in supporting you to develop your mindset and to feel empowered to make positive changes to your practice. You will certainly discover all you need herein to help yourself, your students and your colleagues thrive in higher education and the wider world.

Go on, turn the page, liberate that transformative thought, and begin your own personal journey.

Dr Jennifer Hill
Professor of Higher Education Pedagogies
Head of Learning and Teaching Innovation
University of Gloucestershire

Introduction

Welcome to *The Flourishing Student*

Are you an academic or professional member of staff in a Higher Education (HE) institution?

Did you choose this profession because you saw it as an opportunity for sharing your passion for a subject or field with young people who will become the future workers, citizens and leaders?

Do you believe in making a positive contribution to young people's lives by helping your students to become culturally literate, intellectually reflective and committed to lifelong learning?

Are you keen to empower them to interact socially and respectfully with others and their communities and to possess all the core skills, competencies and habits required to become a confident and engaged adult, citizen and employee of the future?

Have you been wondering what is going on with young people, their mental health and well-being and why they are reporting increasing levels of stress and anxiety and, most importantly, why it does not seem to be improving?

Have you had students come to your office, either very upset or despondent, indicating they felt that they could not achieve any or some of the things mentioned above?

Have you also been discussing your own level of stress, anxiety and general mental health with your colleagues, finding yourself coping with a large amount of work, leaving at the end of each day feeling like you have not achieved all the tasks you had set for yourself?

Has the introduction of new dimensions of online learning in the Covid-19 pandemic raised the bar on levels of stress, anxiety and overwhelm?

Have you wondered how your contribution influences the student–tutor dynamic and learning goals, as a part of the interconnected system of social, neurobiological, ecological and economic components of university life?

If you answered yes to some of these questions, then this book is for you.

Why a book on mental health?

My own personal journey through emotions and challenges awoke in me a real passion for and interest in mental health, well-being and resilience, especially in education, which is the field I have been working in over the last 20 years. This second edition has been an opportunity to sit down and reflect on my journey from when I wrote the first edition of this book in 2017. It draws on all the further interviews, research and conversations I have had on the podcast I created after its first publication, called Flourishing Education.[1] The changes and additions to the content in this new book represent the key take-aways and what are, for me, the most important points to keep in mind as we move forward into the 'new normal' post-Covid.

Why a book on Higher Education in particular?

I worked for two UK universities between 1998 and 2005. My academic background is in linguistics and intercultural competence. I became particularly interested in the linguistic use of negative modifiers when talking about mental health and their impact on our understanding of the notion of mental health, particularly as its use in the English language seems to defer so much to its French equivalent.

I then left for a period of ten years (to have children; to set up and run my business). This entailed training and gaining qualifications as a Mindfulness teacher and hypnotherapist, with a focus on stress and anxiety in education. In 2014, I returned as an academic member of staff at the same UK university I left in 2005 and was taken aback by the changes I noticed in relation to students' well-being. In less than ten years, some students seemed less able to handle the academic work at university, showing lower levels of subjective well-being, more stress and anxiety, and telling me that they felt less able to perform tasks that their peers could do nine years ago. My tutees regularly report that their number-one stressor is the academic workload, even though the workload itself has not increased.

One of my roles as an academic personal tutor is to see students from their first to their final year, providing them with academic support and helping them review some of their academic work or develop their academic skills. I am often a 'listening ear' or the first person they come to see when they are experiencing personal and medical difficulties that affect their studies. It was striking the level of emphasis on mental health in their conversations, in particular the mental health problems they had in the past or were experiencing now, as well as their friends.

Since returning to HE, I have also noticed that this emphasis on mental health and mental health problems among students in HE is reflected on social media. The

Guardian has a whole section on its website entitled 'Mental health: a university crisis'.[2] Other media regularly report on the particular crisis in HE.

I started reading articles and became intrigued by the notion of a mental health crisis in education; so much so that I decided to research this concept and interview experts in the field, as well as students who have been diagnosed with a mental disorder or are experiencing mental distress, and colleagues.

As part of this research, I came across Corey Keyes's (2002) concept of 'flourishing and languishing'. He describes the concept of *flourishing* as a life lived with high levels of emotional, psychological and social well-being (p.299). When I interviewed Dr Keyes, he told me that he chose the word flourishing after thinking very deeply about what would be an appropriate concept for mental health that would make it very clear that he was talking about the presence and absence of the good stuff. He also added that, for him, flourishing is the epitome of good mental health. Flourishing individuals have enthusiasm for life, are productively engaged with others and in society, and are resilient in the face of personal challenges. In contrast, a languishing individual is devoid of positive emotion towards life and is not functioning well psychologically (p.299).

The interviews I carried out were initially with ten students from six different institutions throughout the UK about their stories of resilience. This was followed by a further 13 interviews with students studying various subjects such as languages, medicine, engineering and mathematics. These interviews suggest that there is indeed a difference between a *flourishing* and a *languishing* student and that it has an impact on their studies.

Over time, I have developed my own model to describe the *flourishing student* which I call the *Flourishing Model (FM)*. Since its first creation, I have surveyed over 200 young people and also interviewed students and teachers in lower years of the schooling system (mainly secondary school) to deepen my understanding of what makes young people flourish or languish. I have also carried out over 124 interviews (and counting) for the Flourishing Education podcast, focusing on broader conversations about educational transformation of which well-being is a part. The outcome of this work is this second edition you are reading. My wish is that you enjoy reading it as much as I enjoyed researching and writing it!

What is the aim of this book?

When it comes to lecturing, teaching or helping our students, whilst we may hope for the perfect solution, or at least a formula that might help us make the best impact, we acknowledge the inter-individual differences in human biology, conditions and learning behaviours. So rather than 'one size fits all' 'one path for all', it's about discovering the approach that will work best for you as well as your students. It's about **one's path** and **one's size**.

The Flourishing Student is intended as a perfectly imperfect companion in its role to support you as a tutor in understanding mental health in HE. In turn, you can help your students to flourish academically and in all aspects of their university lives, from a cognitive, emotional, physical, social and spiritual perspective. I will expand on this further in the coming chapters, but this is a message I want to be crystal clear on right from the onset. This book will provide you with tips and suggestions on how to supplement your tutoring style and existing knowledge of mental health and mental disorders, learning from your students, especially those who have been able to flourish at university (sometimes despite a huge amount of challenges and adversity) and contribute to their communities. Best practice is shared all the time in the workplace so why aren't students given this opportunity?

This book will show how some students have used their personal experience and interactions and relationships with their personal tutors as the first building block on their path to resilience, which is achieved one brick at a time. Benard (2004, pp.3–4) defines resilience as 'a capacity all youth have for healthy development and successful learning', which should not be seen as a 'personality trait that one either has or does not have, rather than as an innate capacity bolstered by environmental protective factors' (p.9).

It most definitely is a journey with ups and downs for all who are part of this education system. We will all suffer from stress and anxiety at some point in our lives. It's part of being human. Everything in life is transient; our own lives are. I truly hope that this book shines a new light on the concept of mental health and well-being, and that it brings a new perspective that will make you not only reflect but also see how it can be directly applied to your life.

What is this book about?

The aim of this book is threefold so will be split into three parts.

Overall, the focus is on bringing awareness, under-standing and clarity as well as some practical (and optimisti-cally useful) tips around several key elements:

- the language and terminology used around terms such as mental health and well-being and how it affects our construct of these concepts;
- the notion of the normal stresses of life versus mental disorder and illness;
- the need for a new model that looks at students' experience holistically and systemically, not in parts;
- the need for academics and professional members of staff in HE/Further Education (FE) who are non-specialists in this topic to become more aware of their own mental health and well-being and also how their work and contributions can have a positive impact on their students' university lives and experiences;
- the importance of critical systemic thinking and practice to bring about change in our institutions and organizations.

Part I will focus on the language used around mental health and its association with so-called negative words such as 'crisis', 'problems', 'issues' and 'disorders'. Does it have an impact on the way we perceive mental health and mental health issues? It will also focus on describing the differences between the normal response to daily life stresses and challenges and major mental illnesses. This section will demonstrate how mental illnesses differ from normal negative mood disorders created by life events or challenges such as bereavement, loss, illness and relationship issues.

In Part II, we will look at the implications for education and the need for a new model that incorporates all the aspects that make a *flourishing student, one that will help us to think in terms of holism (treating the whole person based on individual differences) versus reductionism (treating the symptoms of an average person in the general population).* With the help of students' personal experiences, I will share my Flourishing Model (FM). This new model focuses on students' combined growth and development, not solely on their mental health but on other aspects to see how these impact their overall university experience. The model also highlights specific skills that a *flourishing student* has been found to possess. As such, it provides the tutor with several tools to help students build a 'toolbox' to learn to flourish or expand their flourishing at university and to enjoy their studies and university life.

The last part of the book, Part III, provides a more specific focus on practical activities that personal academic tutors can apply to help their tutees build their own 'toolkit' for self-management and resilience, enabling them to better navigate the challenges and ups and downs of university life. But it is as important to reflect on your own mental health and see how looking after your mental health and well-being can positively impact your own life and those of your students and tutees. We will go from what Bronfenbrenner (1977) calls the micro level of individuals (students and staff) to the meso (systems such as departments, faculties and universities as a whole) as well as the macro level (broader societal constructs) to see how the environment we evolve in shapes our thinking, emotions and actions. We will finish with suggestions on 'what's next' for the future of education, particularly in the ongoing 'new normal' post-Covid. This final section will share ideas and suggestions for a more systems-thinking approach to change in education.

Who is this book for?

It is aimed at anyone who would like to gain a deeper understanding of how stress and anxiety can manifest among the student population in HE settings. It is specifically aimed at all academics and professional members of staff in HE institutions who view themselves as 'non-experts' or who wish to augment existing knowledge on these topics to increase clarity. That said, many parents, young people, as well as teachers and educators in secondary school settings, have also enjoyed reading the first edition.

Disclaimer:

This book and the advice provided is NOT aimed at students who suffer from significant and long-term mental disorders or mental health problems which may be under specific professional and specialist treatments (see Chapter 2 for further details). If we take the analogy of a 'personal trainer', you will be providing your students with advice and tips on how to 'flourish' in terms of mental health, in the same way that a personal trainer would advise a client on how to become physically 'fitter' or to include exercise protocols in their life to improve physical health. But, just like a personal trainer would never tell their client what to do if they had a physical illness or a medical condition and would always advise them to consult the relevant health practitioner, under UNDER NO CIRCUMSTANCES is this book intended to provide medical advice to students. Students who have physical or mental ill-health or who suffer from serious diagnosed mental health problems need to be referred to the relevant professionals so that they receive the health care most relevant and adapted to their needs. If in any doubt, the relevant well-being and health services within your institution are best equipped to support students or to refer them on to other services, particularly during challenging situations, difficult times or when they are at crisis point.

How to use this book

Unless you already have a great understanding and knowledge of stress and anxiety, mental health issues and disorders in HE settings, I would suggest that you start at the beginning of the book. Many people who read the first edition of this book have told me how useful the beginning section has proved to them and how refreshing it was to have a clear definition of terminology we use daily in our professional lives and beyond. This book will remind you of the importance of putting your own oxygen mask on first, so to speak, and looking after your own mental health and well-being in the process. To me, this is one of the most vital and important points to take away from this book.

PART I

GAINING UNDERSTANDING AND CLARITY

Chapter 1

Setting the scene

The current state of student mental health in UK Higher Education

'The noblest pleasure is the joy of understanding'
– Leonardo da Vinci

The general picture

To better understand the overall context surrounding UK HE, here are some facts that you might find interesting drawn from Universities UK.

- 2.53 million students were studying in the UK at HE level in 2019/20.[3] Between 2018/19 and 2019/20, the total number of student enrolments increased by 3% and the number of first-year postgraduate taught students increased by 10%.
- 56.9% (1.44 million) were female, 42.6% (1.09 million) male and 0.15% (3,865) other.
- Almost 40% of students were aged 20 and under, 29% were aged 21 to 24, 11% were aged between 25 and 29, and 20% were aged 30 and over.

- In 2019/20, the majority studied in England (2.06 million), then Scotland (260,490), Wales (136,355) and finally Northern Ireland (59,075).
- Around 569,000 students lived in rented accommodation, almost 361,000 in accommodation maintained by the institutions, 379,000 at their parental/guardian home, almost 333,000 in their own accommodation and 175,000 in private sector halls.

What about student health?

Mental health problems are a growing public health concern both in the UK and around the world. For example, according to the Mental Health Foundation, the 2014 Adult Psychiatric Morbidity Survey highlights that every week one in six adults in the UK experiences a common health problem such as 'anxiety' or 'depression' and one in five adults has considered taking their own life at some point.[4] At this point, it is of course vital to mention Covid-19 and the huge negative impact it has had on our well-being as a nation. A recent article in the *Lancet* which tracked changes in the mental health of the UK population before the Covid-19 pandemic and during lockdown shows an overall increase in mental distress in people aged 16 years over and older compared with the previous year (in 2019).[5]

The Higher Education landscape – post-Covid

At the end of November 2020, the Office for National Statistics carried out a pilot survey of university students to provide information about student behaviour during the Covid-19 pandemic. More than half of the participants (57%)

reported a worsening of their mental health and well-being and students appeared to be more anxious than the general population of Great Britain.[6]

A study carried out by Cao et al. (2020) showed that about 25% of the students surveyed experienced anxiety linked to worries about academic delays, the economic effects of the pandemic and the impact on daily life.

Eighty-three per cent of the participants in a survey by YoungMinds (2020) agreed that their pre-existing symptoms of mental health conditions worsened because of the pandemic due to school closures, loss of routine and lack of social connections.[7]

Whether or not you have been working in the HE sector, I am sure you are acutely aware that the important topics of student 'mental health' and 'mental health problems' have regularly appeared in our media over the years. When I wrote the first edition of this book, I found many articles suggesting that stress is much more prevalent than we think. For example, a survey carried out in 2013 by a private insurance company, entitled 'The Aviva Health of the Nation Index', reported that GPs are spending a lot more time dealing with mental health issues.[8] It is the most prevalent type of illness, with the study reporting that 84% of GPs are seeing more patients than ever before suffering from stress and anxiety. Conversations with a GP working at a student health service confirmed this; they described their work as 'trying to close the stable door after the horse has bolted'.

A survey carried out by the National Union of Students (NUS) in 2020 revealed that over half of students (52%) have worse mental health than before the Covid-19 pandemic.[9] During lockdown, many reported having insufficient contact with others: two in five of the students in a relationship reported never seeing their partner, whilst only 13% saw their friends more than once a week. Interestingly, whilst half the students indicated that they were interacting more with family, they also said that contact with other support networks had decreased. 57% of students interacted less frequently with other students at their institution, 53% less with friends and 65% less with clubs and societies. Given the importance of social health for humans and mammals, this clearly impacted on young people's mental health (and to the same extent on adults too).

Research has clearly shown that many of the major mental illnesses begin to appear during adolescence and early adulthood; 50% of mental health problems are established by age 14 and 75% by age 24.[10] It is thus important to not only bring awareness to mental health and mental illnesses/disorders but also cultivate a clear understanding of what constitutes a mental disorder/illness so that everyone in education (staff, parents and students alike) has the right knowledge, competences and attitudes to help themselves and others, if needed.

As pointed out by Dr Stan Kutcher in a recent article in the *Saltwire*: 'Mental illnesses are drivers of suicide, lead to shortened life expectancy, increase risk for other chronic diseases (e.g. diabetes, heart disease) and can negatively impact personal, social and economic success.' We also need to recognize that 'despite over a decade of mental health awareness building, rapid access to best evidence-based mental health care for young people is not where it needs to be.'[11]

I share Kutcher's view that we must do a better job of focusing on mental illness as well as addressing mental health. We need to focus on pathogenesis (an understanding of what causes a mental illness and what treatments we can provide for said illnesses) so that we can prevent mental illness at a population level.

In the past, the key focus has been on treating mental disorders and challenges, as well as fixing dysfunction. Science has been trying to tackle the problem of mental illness by mirroring our approach to physical illnesses and disorders, focusing on the causes of pathological states or abnormal states. A focus on a positive approach to mental health is not the sole answer either. Perhaps the answer needs to be more nuanced and balanced. When I interviewed Professor Corey Keyes on the Flourishing podcast (Episode 4), he told me that at the public health level we also need to take a salutogenic approach, which focuses on what promotes the well-being and health of human beings as well as protects against the loss of well-being.[12] If we were to put those two systems in place, we would move towards the complete health paradigm. We could get our population to that sweet spot of more people flourishing and being free of mental health disorders; this really appeals to me.

I am not a mental health expert nor a specialist in mental ill-health. I am an educator and teacher. My work and research have been focused on something different: on how young people and staff can flourish and maintain their well-being. The aim and focus of this book will be on flourishing education or the ultimate development and functioning of individuals, communities and institutions.

Why are students reporting getting increasingly stressed?

The general labelling in the media of university being the best time of students' lives may not be true for every student. Some of the young people I interviewed told me that they found this idea 'extremely jarring and upsetting because it makes us *feel inadequate and like we are doing something wrong. Why are we not enjoying ourselves when it's supposed to be the best years of our lives?'*

When I interviewed students, it became clear that many of them experience a real period of transition when they move to a new city and enrol at university for the first year of their degree. It is a transition between adolescence and adulthood. It is also a transition between dependence and independence, in a new environment, away from the safety and security of home. They consider the staff members in the departments/schools where they study as their main points of contact. They rely on us as adults to provide them with advice and guidance.

Have you ever wondered why so many students say that they feel stressed? A lot of current research explores the reasons behind this increased self-reported stress and anxiety among students. It is a complex and multifaceted issue with no single answer. One student I interviewed summarized it beautifully when she said:

There are problems everywhere. It's a generation issue – where we are surrounded by problems with the media telling us that we should all be slimmer and what diet to follow – what degree to do to earn a lot of money, what to look like and how to succeed and even how to choose a boyfriend. Your job and your career say everything about you. It's not the same values as one or two generations before. As a result, when you go to university, you are not just there to study, you are there to make friends, to be popular, to be known and so if those aren't happening, you question yourself.

This statement clearly highlights the complexity of the issue and all the challenges, academic but also personal and social, that students are faced with when they join a HE institution and embark on their degree. Below is a list of some of the specific points highlighted by students in previous research and drawn from my own interviews:

- *Academic workload*

Many of my students regularly cite workload as their number-one stressor. Research seems to confirm this with large-scale studies of the major stressors of the first year indicating that students cannot handle the academic work (Sax 1997). Yet, this workload has not changed and is not more demanding than in previous years.

- *Concerns about the future*

These concerns include the 'doom and gloom' stories in the press and on social media about the impact of Brexit, Covid and climate change, for example. Uncertainty and fear of something going wrong in the future all contributes to the automatic nervous system kicking in (we will read more about this in Chapter 2 about stress). Much research has been carried out on the impact of climate change on young people's mental health. A recent article in *Nature* explains how young people are experiencing 'eco-anxiety', distress and anger at the way the issues around climate change are being dealt with by governments and societies.[13] This is a cause of great concern (and understandably so) for young people who worry about the future of the blue planet as well as theirs.

- *Exams and assessments*

A survey called 'Silently Stressed' carried out by NUS Scotland, based on 1,800 students from 19 FE colleges and 15 universities across Scotland, found that 90% of students reported that exams and assessments caused them more stress than anticipated; only 2% said they experienced no stress at all.[14] Some of my tutees are unable to revise because of stress; they procrastinate and leave their work until the last minute, which creates even more stress as the deadline approaches and they realize they will not be able to meet it.

- *Extrinsic instead of intrinsic motivation*

Several students mentioned that they felt that they had chosen to come to university for 'extrinsic' reasons: to earn their degree (with a good classification) so that they could get a good well-paid job that would help them to lead a comfortable life. One student in particular said to me:

> *I am in my final year so I am not going to stop now but after having therapy and discussing my situation, I now realize that I shouldn't have come to university because I didn't have enough of an internal desire to engage and participate in university life fully because I found it personally rewarding or enjoyable. I did because that's what my parents and teachers expected from me and encouraged me to do and I didn't want to upset them. I was also worried that I would not be able to find a job otherwise.*

He added: '*Society says that young people need a degree to get a good job, earn good money and be happy but I am not sure that's true.*'

• *Financial worries*

The increase in university fees and financial worries have featured regularly in the press. Students regularly mention that they must pay £9,250 per year to attend university. The substantial debt after a three- or four-year degree programme is a clear source of anguish for young people, who worry about starting their working life with such a large amount of money to pay off.

The impact of financial concerns on overall mental health has become a popular topic among researchers and practitioners. For example, Roberts et al. (2000) identified a link between the adverse financial situations of college students and the negative impact on mental and physical health that translated into mental distress. Andrews and Wilding (2004) found that financial stressors were positively associated with increased anxiety and depression levels among college students in the United Kingdom.

• *Future careers*

In the same survey by Andrews and Wilding (2004), over 75% of students reported that thinking about their future career prospects after graduation was reasonably or very stressful. Some students I interviewed said that this was linked to the pressure of exams and assessments: they believe that they must perform well to get the best job possible when they leave university. These feelings are compounded by media reports suggesting that specific degrees will help students to earn the largest amounts of money.

- *Happiness and unrealistic expectations*

I recently surveyed over 200 parents for research on my third book. A common sentiment was: '*I want my child(ren) to be happy.*' As a mother, I completely understand where this stems from. Of course, we would all like to see our children lead happy lives. The media and our society also suggest to young people that by getting ahead, achieving good grades and reaching their goals and outcomes, they will be happy. My take on this is that it unfortunately creates an unachievable target. It also sends the message that happiness can be maintained or reached as an end point, and that there is something wrong when young people experience 'negative or unhappy emotions'. We will discuss this further when we look at language and also in Chapter 4.

- *Poor diet/reduced physical activity*

We will see in Part II how important our physical health is for our overall well-being. The students I spoke to as part of the research highlighted the fact that they felt much better after doing some sport (as part of the numerous clubs offered in their institution) or if they went for a walk or a run. A growing body of evidence indicates that physical activity and fitness can benefit both the health and academic performance of students and so does eating a healthy and balanced diet.

- *Pressure to perform – get a 2:1 or preferably a first*

Students put a lot of pressure on themselves and have high expectations. Aspiration is a good thing and why wouldn't we want to have goals or outcomes for the future? There's absolutely no issue with aiming high but young people are driven by success at all costs; they think the most important thing is to gain a 2:1 or a first so that they can get a good well-paying job and clear their debts. This is obvious when we provide students with feedback or discuss points about exams: many students seem to be mainly motivated by the mark rather than the feedback which will help them to improve and progress.

- *Relationship difficulties*

Some of the students I interviewed explained that whilst they mostly enjoy their relationships with their parents, friends, flatmates or their boyfriends/girlfriends, at times these relationships created some stress and anxiety because they sometimes 'went wrong'. During the Covid-19 pandemic, this aspect was heavily discussed and highlighted, as indicated earlier in this section when I mentioned the recent NUS survey. Our relationship issues heavily impact our mental health and well-being. For example, in the first lockdown, the UK National Domestic Abuse Helpline reported a 25% increase in calls and online requests for support.[15]

- *Social media and use of technology*

Social media and the use of technology have clearly improved our lives, enabling us to connect with people on the other side of the planet. The Internet enables us to get information almost instantly and to raise awareness of political and social issues. In many ways, it has brought us many positives but we also tend to spend a lot of time on social media or connected via our phones and other electronic gadgets.

Researchers have recently shown that social media and being constantly connected has a negative impact on our lives, ranging from insomnia to depression. A student I interviewed said that he had to delete Facebook from his phone and computer because he had become addicted and spent too much time checking his newsfeed/comments about his status. He also said that he worried about what others thought of his photos and comments and regularly had to ask friends to comment on or like his posts to help him feel less self-conscious.

During Covid-19 and because of the different lockdowns, many young people experienced 'Zoom fatigue' resulting from many hours studying online using the same technology. Covid-19 has also highlighted the deeply seated inequalities in society; research has shown the magnified socio-technical discrepancies between individuals. Many young people found themselves without access to technology during the pandemic: either because they had no computer or had Internet connection difficulties (e.g. in rural areas), or because multiple people in their household required Internet access.

- *Substance misuse*

Some students I interviewed reported using some substances excessively to get through the day (drugs but also alcohol, caffeine supplements, prescription drugs as well as energy drinks). In a recent interview, a student told me how their best friend had written their whole final-year essay under the influence of speed because *'they felt they couldn't tap into their creativity and found that was the only way to let go of their worries and to allow their thoughts on the topic to flow freely'*. Bennett and Holloway (2013) found widespread drug misuse on a university campus in terms of the types and patterns of misuse.

- *Impact of overparenting*

This is also known as helicopter parenting and involves high parental expectations (Cline and Fay 1990; Munich and Munich 2009). These parenting practices reduce demands on children to undertake behaviours that would effect change in their own lives (Locke et al. 2012). The main issue with helicopter parenting is that it does not teach students to learn from their mistakes and become independent. As a result, students increasingly say: *'I can't do it, do it for me.'*

- *Transition from secondary school to university*

This includes issues of coping with independent living and life at university. Hughes (2012) explains that the transition to HE can be a stressful experience, often resulting in psychological distress, anxiety, depression, sleep disturbance, reduction in self-esteem and isolation. He also adds that the transition has been found to play a key role in student suicide.

According to Richardson et al. (2012), the first year of university study is one of the most significant transition periods in a student's life. They must learn new academic skills as well as new social and independent living skills. For many students, the struggle to balance the competing demands of study, work and personal commitments feels overwhelming and they report significant declines in their overall health and well-being.

Some of the students I interviewed also clearly stated that they found their experience at university challenging because they didn't feel they had the skills required to tackle some of the tasks set in their first year at university. Listening to their stories, some students seem to have difficulties dealing with the academic workload because it is so different from their A levels, where their work is 'chunked down' into 'bitesize bits' that they 'digest' and 'regurgitate' to get the grades they need for their GCSEs and A levels. Several students explained that their tutors had been there 'every step of the way' and that they were always told 'what to do next'. This is clearly required by secondary schools (and more and more primary schools) because of the pressure on members of staff (with performance-related pay) and schools (for funding) to ensure that as many students as possible get good grades.

As I write this second edition, I would like to focus for a little bit longer on this last point and add some further thoughts that have only become obvious to me since Covid happened. Whilst there is no real scope in this book to develop this fully, I want to reinforce and reiterate my feelings that in HE settings we are 'firefighting' at the receiving end of a schooling system that fosters competitiveness and individualism in the name of high attainment. Over the last four years, I have not only worked with A-level students to understand what their key pressure points are, but have also interviewed over one hundred individuals as part of the Flourishing Education podcast. This has been a common theme in many of those conversations. The current focus in the English education system on achieving high grades for what are considered 'high-stakes' exams (GCSEs and A levels), and the constant prior testing or 'mock examining' is indeed generating extremely high levels of stress for young people. Is it therefore surprising that our children and young people in HE are stressed out and anxious? We will discuss chronic stress later in the book but many young people are clearly continuously in fear. One student I interviewed told me:

> *There is nowhere to go to escape this pressure. It comes from teachers, my headteacher during assemblies and even from my own parents who tell me that I won't lead a successful life if I don't have these important exams under my belt.*

The interviews my colleague Dr Dominique Thompson and I carried out to write our book *How to Grow a Grown Up* also showed us that young people develop a fear of failure, perfectionism, an imposter syndrome as well as what I call 'comparatitis' – the need to compare themselves to others (negatively). In fact, fear of failure has sadly been reported as being a particular British trend for our children and young people, which makes them, it would appear, the most unhappy teenagers in Europe.[16]

Mental health – a definition

'Mental health' is a mass noun and the Oxford Dictionary describes it as 'a person's condition with regard to their psychological and emotional well-being'.

The World Health Organization (WHO) defines mental health as a 'state of well-being in which every individual realizes his or her own potential, can cope with the normal stresses of life, can work productively and fruitfully, and is able to make a contribution to her or his community' (WHO 2004).

Once again, the above definitions raised many questions for me as a linguist. You will no doubt agree with me that they are very positive and empowering definitions. So, why are we not seeing these used in the press and media more often, with that positive sense of 'state of mental well-being' just like we see the word physical health on its own as meaning a 'state of physical well-being'?

How can we explain the discrepancies between these positive definitions and the current loaded and negative connotations of the term 'mental health'? Is it solely because of the use of negative modifiers alongside it? Why are we using negative modifiers with such a positively charged word? Why are we not provided with the positive definitions more often as they seem so much more empowering?

The confusing impact of multiple negative modifiers

The following terms are used regularly in the press and during our conversations:

Mental health condition	Mental illness	Mental health disorder
Mental health issue	Mental health crisis	Mental health problem
Mental health illness	Mental ill-health	Mental disorder

Confused already? So was I when I first started researching the topic of 'mental health'.

All of the terms listed in the table carry negative connotations that seem to reinforce the 'wrongness' and 'badness' of the state of one's mind. They are also all used intermittently and interchangeably as meaning the same thing, creating semantic confusion. When young people and non-experts in the field use the language, they are now confusing 'mental health' with 'mental disorder'.

It is vital to bring back some clarity around the negative linguistic uses of 'mental health' because, as demonstrated by the experiment 'Do words hurt?' (2010) carried out by Maria Richter and other colleagues who monitored their participants' brain responses to auditory and imagined negative words, painful or negative words release stress and anxiety-inducing hormones in subjects.

The authors of *Words Can Change Your Brain*, Andrew Newberg and Mark Robert Waldman, write that 'a single word has the power to influence the expression of genes that regulate physical and emotional stress' (p.25). We will discuss this further when we talk about 'epigenetics'. But for now, suffice to say that how we talk, think and feel about a concept such as 'mental health' clearly impacts our subjective response.

We thus need to pay closer attention to the words we use, especially when we talk about mental health – not just because it will have an impact on us but also because, as a linguist, I am convinced that muddled language will lead to muddled thinking.

With this second edition of the book, I would like us to linger on language. I wrote the above in 2017 and today things remain unchanged; if I am completely honest, it really saddens me. There is still too much confusion. I still believe very strongly that in England when we use the word 'mental health' we mean 'mental ill-health' but we don't say this openly. This clearly makes things even more confusing.

I also feel that the words we use have been put in a bag and shaken about: we clearly are all a bit confused (and hugely concerned) when we talk about mental health. I don't feel we are singing from the same hymn sheet, which clearly affects and shapes our response. The next sections will attempt to bring more clarity.

Beforehand though, I'd like to set you a little challenge: Can I invite you to consciously reflect on your own use of these words, and most importantly share this with others so that we can truly start changing how we view 'mental health'?

Why so much negativity?

The use of these negative modifiers suggests that negative information tends to influence evaluations more strongly than comparably positive information around the topic of 'mental health'.

Cacioppo et al. (1997) describe it as 'negativity bias'. In one of Cacioppo's studies, his conclusions were that our brains demonstrate more responsivity to negative stimuli than positive stimuli. Negative stimuli generate a greater surge in electrical activity. As a result, our attitudes and behaviours are more strongly influenced by negative input than positive input (Cacioppo et al. 1994).

Cacioppo also suggests that the negative bias coincides with Cannon's (1929) notion that threatening stimuli are more likely to elicit general and diffuse sympathetic activation as part of an adaptive fight-or-flight response which emphasizes the relative impact of negative information on our actions.

To keep us safe, our nervous system has therefore designed ways to make it impossible for us to miss possible dangers and threats and therefore respond to them. We will see how important and relevant this concept is when we discuss the 'fight-or-flight response' in Chapter 2.

Is this why we tend to focus on the negatives? Is it a way to feel in control of potential problems, to solve them and quite literally stay alive? This would also explain why we tend to focus on the pathogenic and the concept of mental ill-health rather than on how to support and maintain our levels of well-being.

Research highlights that we generally need more positives to balance out the negatives. In a 2000 article, Fredrickson et al. showed that the balance between positive and negative emotions contributes to our judgement of life satisfaction and that emotions alter our thinking and actions. This is particularly relevant to informing conversations around the negativity surrounding 'mental health'.

Rozin and Royzman (2001) also consider the contagiousness of negative events as the primary reason for their strength and dominance. This may explain why there has been such a rise in reports of stress and anxiety. The student responses during our interviews seem to corroborate this concept: students stated that reading articles or hearing stories of other people having a difficult time and being stressed made them much more aware of their own problems. This left them with the feeling that *'Yes, that's me. I think I am also experiencing these issues or this extreme level of stress.'*

Language is obviously a vital tool. Not only does it help us communicate our thoughts and ideas but it also helps us connect with others and create cultural ties, friendships and relationships. So, let's see why the language we use around mental health matters. We will then tackle the specific language uses around mental health in Chapter 2.

The language we use matters

The danger of labelling oneself and others

Have you ever heard a joke about someone with cancer or made a casual reference to someone with high blood pressure; have you ever teased anyone by saying that he's got diabetes? I'd say this would be very unlikely because we don't tend to make much fun of someone for having a physical illness. In fact, we tend to have a lot of empathy for people who are 'physically' unwell or ill. But in our society, some people never give a second thought to making comments about others having 'mental illnesses'. Have you ever used, or heard used, the terms 'psycho', 'schizo' or 'bipolar' or even that someone is 'mental' or 'OCD'? These words tend to be used almost automatically in daily conversation without having a full understanding of their meaning. This has a significant impact on how we perceive 'mental health' and 'mental disorders', increasing the stigma around these topics. By using these words with the verb 'to be', we give people who experience them an identity or a label. The problem with identities and labels is that they can lead to a feeling of permanence and, as one student indicated, 'that we may be stuck with' for the rest of our lives.

Interestingly, a colleague and I were recently commenting that we don't do this semantically with physical ill-health. We would say 'I suffer from cancer' not 'I am cancer'. We would never say 'I am broken foot' or 'I am broken arm' but we say 'I am depressed'. Wouldn't it be beneficial to consider this further? Maybe this would help us view our mental illnesses in the same light as a physical illness? I would love nothing more than this so that we can end the stigma around mental ill-health and bring 'parity of esteem' between mental health and physical health. We know we can recover from a physical illness or learn to live well with a physical illness; perhaps we can also recover from a mental illness or learn to live well with it rather than it being something we 'are' and cannot change. This would give those who currently suffer from mental ill-health hope. Dr Benjamin Hardy, author of *Personality Isn't Permanent*, explains that many of us tend to believe our personalities are fixed and we cannot change them. This is the basis of personality tests determining our 'baseline' personality. But we are constantly evolving and changing. Dr Hardy argues that we change a lot and are very different from the people we were six months or even two years ago. This is why I absolutely love attending the students' graduation ceremony. The individual receiving their degree is definitely not the same individual who first arrived at university. If you want to read more about this, I highly recommend Dr David Eagleman's book *Livewired: The Inside Story of the Ever-Changing Brain*, which explains this from a neuroscientific perspective.

The difference between behaviour and identity

When I talked to students, there seemed to be a clear confusion where students mistook their behaviour – what they do when they are upset or what is happening in a particular environment – for who they are and their identity. As we have seen before, there is a big difference between what we do and who we are. If we start 'confusing' one for the other or 'labelling' ourselves as 'depressed' or 'stressed', it becomes much more difficult to remove this label. For example, one student told me that he was feeling upset because his grandmother died and that as a result he was depressed. This example highlights the fact that we use the terminology 'I am depressed' to talk about a sad event or a sad feeling we experience (here the death of a close relative) but this does not necessarily mean that we 'are depressed' or more exactly that we are suffering from depression; instead, we are experiencing grief and sadness at the loss of a much-loved family member.

Here is another example that I hope will show the difference between behaviour and identity. Imagine that you have a student who is enjoying studying, and is engaged and learning. They are working hard, studying, doing their homework. For intrinsic reasons, the student is motivated to undertake the task for the sake of it rather than because they are gaining good marks; however, their hard work and effort means they are doing well academically and getting good marks. As teachers and parents, we would of course be proud of their 'behaviour' and what they are doing. But very often, instead of saying so: 'I can see how hard you are working', or 'I can see you are doing well', we tend to automatically move up to the identity level and say 'how clever are you', 'you are so bright', 'you are so intelligent', 'I can see how academically minded you are and how good you are at studying'.

However, this could have a very damaging effect (and we will see again why in Part III) because if the student changes their 'behaviour' and stops working as hard, their marks and learning might decrease. Some students may then change their identity and suddenly believe that they are not 'clever enough'. This has been confirmed several times by my tutees who got a 2:2 mark when they first started university, coming to see me in floods of tears because they believed that they were not 'clever enough to be studying here'. One can clearly understand how upsetting this would be for a student if they had been labelled 'clever', 'bright' and 'intelligent' in primary and secondary school because they got straight As or A*s; they could easily mistake their 2:2 mark for an indication of how 'incapable' they are. It is easier to change what we do than to change who we are, our identity which is at the core of our 'persona'. As personal tutors and members of university staff, it is important to be aware of the language we use when we talk to students to avoid 'strengthening' or 'anchoring' the belief that a student's behaviour defines who they are.

Well-being and the concept of 'embedding well-being in the curriculum'

Interestingly, the last couple of years has seen a natural (and sharp) move away from the use of 'mental health' to the concept of 'well-being'. Perhaps because deep down many of us and feel that there is still a lot of confusion around 'mental health' and a lot of stigma around 'mental ill-health'? Perhaps it's a way to steer the conversation in a new direction and start approaching things differently?

The term well-being is increasingly used in our institutions and by colleagues (as well as students). Whilst I agree that it is positive to use a new terminology, the linguist in me also feels strongly about the importance of defining it so that we can be sure that we are all singing from the same hymn sheet when we use it.

Well-being is defined by the Oxford Dictionary as: 'the state of being or doing well in life; happy, healthy, or prosperous condition; moral or physical welfare (of a person or community)'.[17]

The Epicurean hedonic tradition of emotional well-being, also described as feeling good or pleasure, life satisfaction or happiness with our lives, was first introduced to the field of psychology by Ed Diener in the early 1980s. This was well reflected in research on subjective well-being (SWB) and for a long time there was a lot of research on life satisfaction and emotional happiness. In their 2008 paper, Ryan and Deci explained that SWB was widely linked to happiness. Along came Carol Riff, who in an 1989 article published in the *Journal of Personality and Social Psychology* introduced the Aristotelian notion of a good life, functioning well and excellence at being an individual, also known as eudaimonic well-being. Waterman (1993) described it as being concerned with living well or actualizing our human potentials.

Further research now suggests that considering how an individual views well-being is extremely important. Considering well-being through the eudaimonic lens is more robustly associated with self-reported well-being than through the hedonic lens (McMahan and Estes 2011).

Could this explain why so many young people who are searching for the next source of pleasure or satisfaction (by getting the best grade, the next qualification, etc.) are also experiencing a lower level of subjective well-being? Is this pursuit of happiness leaving us frustrated and wanting more, aimlessly looking for the next goal or source of happiness without truly enjoying the journey there? I will be happy when… I get the degree, the good job, the first flat or house, the car, etc. This can be exemplified by the comment a final-year student made whilst waiting for their final-year degree results: '*I really hope that I get my first to compensate for the*

last four years of misery.' My heart literally sank when I heard
them say this. We make a sacrifice to attain the ultimate goal
which might never happen for us because of the fragility of
life, as highlighted by Covid (and personally by the recent
death of my father-in-law).

Are we constantly chasing the next big thing, hoping that
we will be happy? Research shows that although our levels
of happiness are affected by positive or negative events in
our lives, we quickly adapt back to our previous levels. This
is known as 'hedonic adaptation'. So, for example, when we
get a pay rise, we quickly adapt to the increased amount of
money and modify our way of life accordingly. But does this
make us happier as a result? It would seem not. If so, is this
constant search for the next source of pleasure, joy or enjoyment futile?

Beyond these questions, it would be useful to ask ourselves
how we would define happiness and to find out what we view
as a source of happiness. Do we, like the Greek philosopher
Epicurus, believe that happiness is the goal in itself and the
greater the extent of pleasures, the better? Or do we, like Aris-
totle, believe happiness is the by-product of finding activities
or actions that make us feel like we are fulfilling our potential
and give us a purpose for living?

In their article 'The challenge of defining wellbeing', Dodge
et al. (2012) explain how interesting and surprising it is that
despite all the years of research, the focus has been on exploring
the various dimensions of well-being but not on providing
a clear definition. In their paper, they set out to change this,
providing a definition that I really like: they suggest that we
define well-being as 'the balance point between an individual's
resource pool and the challenges faced'. They add that 'stable
wellbeing is when individuals have the psychological, social

and physical resources they need to meet a particular psychological, social and/or physical challenge' (p.229). I will mention the notion of continuum or see-saw dip in Part II, when I introduce the concept of flourishing and languishing, but to me it is a really useful and clear way to highlight and understand 'when individuals have more challenges than resources, the see-saw dips, along with their wellbeing, and vice-versa' (p.230). As my friend, colleague and researcher Natalie Rothwell-Warn says: 'imagine a ball on a seesaw, that's your wellbeing – your challenges are on the left and the resources on the right (or vice-versa). When balanced, this provides you with good well-being. If your challenges become too high though and you don't have enough resources the ball rolls off, putting well-being in a "lost" place because the challenges are too overwhelming for us to cope with.' That's how we can represent the loss of well-being. I really like this simple way of representing well-being: I hope it will help you visualize your own well-being as much as it helped me.

So what about the notion of 'embedding well-being in the curriculum'? For me, this is not about sending individuals (students or staff) on courses to develop their resource pools or their 'toolbox' of resources. It is not tokenism.

Embedding well-being goes much deeper than this, forming part of everything we do in our daily teaching or working activities. One could argue that well-being forms part of the culture of the organization and the way we think. Most importantly, well-being needs to be included in our thinking and approach to planning, teaching as well as assessments.

My colleague Stephanie Demont and I have done quite extensive work on this concept of embedding well-being in the French language curriculum. Through our research, we have discovered that there are five key elements that foster well-being, which are drawn from research by Larcombe et al. (2017), Bandura, as well as Deci and Ryan (Self-Determination Theory). At the centre is autonomous motivation, also known as intrinsic motivation. This drives all of our actions. When we want to do something or feel inspired to explore a new subject, for example, we display what is called intrinsic motivation. The other side of the coin is called extrinsic motivation (or carrots and sticks), which requires others to motivate us to do something. When our children are small, we use a technique known as operant conditioning attributed to Skinner;[18] this is achieved by giving them stickers or reward charts when we like what they are doing and by punishing them or telling them off when we don't like what they are doing. The issue I have with such techniques is that when you remove the carrots or sticks, individuals don't always know what to do nor how to tap into their intrinsic motivation.

After motivation come sense of belonging and positive relationships. These two are easy to explain; we have previously discussed what their absence does to our well-being and how it affects it negatively. As mammals we flourish when socially engaged with others. The fourth element is a sense of autonomy and finally the fifth is self-efficacy, or the sense of competence that emerges as we develop mastery, skills and knowledge in a certain area. Our research on the French curriculum has shown that it is possible to help students develop their sense of autonomy, belonging and to support them in building strong and positive relationships with their tutors and peers.

Autonomous motivation and sense of competence, however, seem to be strongly linked and much more difficult to achieve when supporting young people. When we reach a plateau in our learning, when we believe we have all the answers, that decreases our motivation. Equally, when we realize how much there is to learn still, it can frighten us. If we accept that there is something to learn and don't equate failure (at understanding a new concept, grasping a particular idea for example) with being a failure, which we know is a very common feature in young people's lives, will we see a difference in approach to both motivation and sense of competence? This clearly requires more time to be researched, as indicated in the article we recently wrote.[19]

If you are particularly interested in this topic, you may want to check out this QAA collaborative project which explores how mental well-being can be embedded into all aspects of higher education to enhance the student experience.[20]

One final point: well-being/mental fitness clearly are not only about the individual – we all influence each other's well-being through our interactions and relationships. As you read this book, I invite you to think about your own well-being and how it is impacted by others and the relationships and communities in which you engage, and then in turn how your well-being impacts others.

Chapter 2

Time for clarity and understanding

A real need for mental health literacy

*'Clarity, clarity, surely clarity is the most beautiful
thing in the world'*
– George Oppen

What is stress?

After a hard day at work where we constantly answer requests from others via emails or face to face, without mentioning some of the issues we have to deal with in the office with our colleagues and at home with our partners and children, we often say that we are feeling 'stressed'. It is a sensation that so many students report experiencing on a regular basis.

But what do we mean exactly when we say that we are 'stressed'?

The impressions and situations that can generate some stress can be different for every individual. When I asked students about this topic, they most commonly stated that they were feeling stressed because they felt powerless and didn't have the resources to fight against or to master a situation.

Remember: We can feel stressed because we feel that we are incapable of mastering, dealing with or controlling a situation.

Stress affects our body and mind in several ways. First of all, it creates a complex physiological reaction. But what if we considered it for what it is? A natural response of the body, also known as the term fight/flight, from the sympathetic nervous system. This survival mechanism, also called hyperarousal or acute stress response, was first coined by Walter Bradford Cannon in his two books *Bodily Changes in Pain, Hunger, Fear, and Rage* (1915) and *Wisdom of the Body* (1932).

Our brains react quickly to keep us safe by preparing the body for action. Just like animals, humans react to acute stress by either fighting the threat, freezing or fleeing from it. It is a healthy survival mechanism to put our bodies on full alert in case we need to run away or suddenly need a lot of strength to save our life. It is there to protect us. Most of the fears that plague us today exist only in our imagination: they are not real threats. But the amygdala cannot tell the difference so the nervous system gets stuck in unnecessary stress responses. This primitive mechanism is called the 'system of defensive behaviour' (LeDoux 1998). Defence against danger, LeDoux argues, is probably the number-one priority of any organism.

Key points to remember

This 'fight, flight or freeze' response is there because it prepares us to either fight or run away to escape the danger, but if neither of these two options works and it seems like we are going to be killed by our predator, then we go into a shock state known as tonic immobility. We do this because we are in a state of fear. This tonic immobility is well documented in animals and we can see it when a cat catches a mouse, which then starts playing dead and does not move.

In *Making the World Safe for Our Children* (2015), Professor Steve Porges, who created the polyvagal theory, helps us understand how 'cues of risk and safety, consciously monitored by our nervous system, influence physiological and behavioural states' (p.221). His work provides extremely useful information on the 'freeze response'.[21] The defensive mode of freeze in fear is in fact 'shutting down, passing out or in dissociative states' Through his work, we now have a clearer understanding of this 'freeze' state, which is often associated with traumatic events and Post-Traumatic Stress Disorder (PTSD), where many people report feeling dissociated from their emotions and feelings. We will describe the stress response in more details in the next section but for now suffice to say that this fight, flight or freeze response is a fast and automatic 'gearing up', which can prove essential when we are faced with danger. As explained before, this is what enabled our ancestors in more primitive times to survive when we were constantly faced with threatening situations: we either fought a sabretooth tiger or simply ran away from it.

The stress response – what happens in our body

The autonomic nervous system (ANS) is a big network of nerves reaching out from the spinal cord and directly affects every organ in the body. It comprises two branches: the sympathetic and the parasympathetic, which have completely opposite effects. The sympathetic branch triggers the stress response and helps us deal with dangerous or life-threatening situations as an attempt at keeping us alive. Adrenalin is released, which increases our heartbeat and our blood pressure to direct the blood towards numerous muscles so that we can use them to either flight or fight.

Blood is diverted away from the stomach because digestion is not really required in a life-or-death situation. What is the point of digesting your food if you are going to be someone's dinner? Functions considered as non-essential in a fight-or-flight situation are suppressed, such as the ability to reproduce, to grow (for children) or to digest. This also explains why we report feeling 'butterflies in our stomach' or 'feeling sick' when we're stressed. The blood is diverted from the stomach to the muscles and brain to provide them with the energy and oxygen they require.

As a result of this response, we also experience fear and worries. When we are facing a potential physical danger, these emotions motivate us to pay attention to what is going on around us and to take care of ourselves. The sympathetic nervous system is really the 'fear-based system' that is used any time we see an object or an individual as a threat to our survival.

After the danger has passed, the *parasympathetic* ANS takes over, decreasing the heartbeat and relaxing the blood vessels. This helps our bodies to be in a state that supports health, growth and restoration, or the 'rest and digest' mode.

Porges's work emphasizes what he sees as the human quest to calm neural defence systems by detecting features of safety' (p.221). When we feel safe, we feel able to spontaneously engage with others. He calls this system the 'social engagement system', which is closely linked to the face–heart connection. In the case of the social engagement system, we can rapidly engage with objects and individuals to promote self-soothing and calmer states. I believe this is this part of our nervous system we recruit or 'tap into' when we are flourishing. I call this part the 'love-based system'. I get really excited by this theory because it is empowering. I can connect or reconnect with others. I have a choice rather than feeling powerless in the face of challenges, difficulties and adversities.

In summary: The flight, flight or freeze response is an automatic reaction which forces our body to shift into high gear. As human beings, we are wired to withstand occasional and extreme stress and our bodies can cope with a lot of pressure. When we lead a healthy life, the two branches of our ANS work in harmony and generate action then rest (and relaxation). In fact, our bodies naturally search to get us back into equilibrium, also known as homeostasis achieved through allostasis.

What does this stress response mean for you as an academic member of staff? Can you think of times when you have experienced this 'flight, fight or freeze' response?

The stress response – an issue in the 21st century?

Our reaction to run away or fight in a dangerous situation was extremely useful for our ancestors who needed to protect themselves against predators. However, nowadays, the situations that generate stress are more often linked to psychological threats than physical ones. We don't have to combat or flee even if our bodies are prepared and ready to do so.

Each time we perceive something as a threat, it means that we are more than likely to trigger this automatic response. This reaction is designed for short-term events or situations.

The physiological responses during an acute stress period can be extremely useful in the short term but if the stress becomes chronic, it can be negative for us.

Remember: The fight, flight or freeze response is triggered every time we perceive a threat in our environment. Unfortunately, we cannot change situations and what happens to us in life. What we can change is the way we see these situations, our perception of events. When something challenging happens in our lives, we need to remember that we are not what happens. What we resist persists and what we embrace dissolves.

Stress is often presented as a big and powerful external force that controls us and that we have to constantly fight. It is often presented as an enemy we need to exterminate but what if it isn't a foe and is instead a friend that we need to get to know?

Stress can in fact help us feel more alert and more motivated to get up, practise or get involved with things. It can also help us gain a competitive edge. Stress can also help us prepare, focus and perform to reach the perfect level. It only becomes a real danger for our health when it becomes chronic instead of acute.

As mentioned previously, this book does not address any of the issues of chronic stress or stress generated by trauma or traumatic events. If you are interested in these concepts, I would highly recommend the work of expert Bessel Van Der Kolk, author of *The Body Keeps the Score*.[22]

Remember: Stress can be good for you. For example, it is what gets me into a room full of people to give a presentation or during an interview. Research demonstrates that dealing with short-term stressors or experiencing acute stress typically do not impose a health burden on healthy individuals.

Why stress is good for us

'The truth is that stress doesn't come from circumstances. It comes from our thoughts about our circumstances,' states Andrew Bernstein (2010).

The way we think about stress also influences what happens to us. In her TED Talk, Stanford University psychologist Kelly McGonigal states that throughout her career she has advised her clients to rid stress from their lives because it can have a negative impact on the human body – she has made stress the 'enemy'.[23]

However, recent work by Lauren Wisk, PhD, and her colleagues made her revise her approach to stress. As described in a 2011 American Psychological Association article (Keller et al. 2012), Dr Wisk's team linked survey data on nearly 30,000 US adults to national death records in order to determine the relationship between levels of stress and the perception that stress impacts health and health outcomes. They found that both higher levels of reported stress and the perception that stress affects health were independently associated with worse physical and mental health.

Most strikingly, those who reported a lot of stress and that stress greatly impacted their health had a 43% increased risk of premature death (over an eight-year period), suggesting that how you think about stress matters just as much as how much stress you have. Thinking that stress is harmful could literally kill us in the long run.

When you change your mind about stress, you can change your body's response to stress. McGonigal suggests that when stress is viewed as a positive, something helpful to performance, a person will be able to decrease its negative effects on physical health. McGonigal's suggestion to change our minds may seem easy but as we develop habitual behaviours and thoughts, it may not be as simple and quick to implement.

As human beings, we tend to label what happens to us as 'good' or 'bad'; we often want the good to continue and the bad to go away. Dr Srikumar Rao uses the parabole of 'good thing, good thing who knows' to help us question this dual/ black-and-white way of thinking.[24] Have you ever experienced an event that felt really positive (for example, getting a good job) only to realize that you were not enjoying it after two weeks? Equally, can you think of an event that you initially labelled as extremely negative, only to later realize that it turned out to be positive (not getting a job only to get an even better job offer later on). We tend to believe that we can control what happens to us in life; perhaps by telling young people that there is a set way to learn and know something for sure by going to the back of the book on page X, we are setting them up to experience negative feelings. We cannot control what happens to us in life (even if deep down we admit that we would love to because the fear of uncertainty is really unsettling). But if we are honest with ourselves, would we truly want to know exactly what is going to unfold next?

Many of the young people I interviewed have experienced many challenges in their lives. I don't know anyone who has not. Experiencing challenges in life is a little bit like being ill during childhood. It helps us build our immunity to viruses and colds. I wonder if we could use the same analogy to shift how we view the events in our lives? What if we considered them as a way to develop our strength and ability to cope when the next challenge arises? As parents, we don't like it when our children are ill, but we recognize that in the long run it will help them be healthier. If we tend to overprotect them and remove all obstacles so that they don't experience any challenges in their early formative years, I think it deprives them of developing their 'coping muscles'. Imagine if we locked up every single child in a germ-free room until they were 18 and then opened the door to let them out. What would happen? They wouldn't stand a chance, would they? Let's not do the same for emotional well-being. Yes, it's not great to pick up the pieces when they are upset or heartbroken but sometimes it's important to think about the long-term impact rather than the short-term benefits. Do we want grown-up children or grown-up adults? This isn't easy, of course. It's just something worth considering if we want well and flourishing young people and young adults.

Research has shown that an inability to cope with uncertainty or the notion of being in limbo has a negative impact on our physical and mental well-being.[25] Experts such as Michel Dugas call this 'uncertainty tolerance' or the underlying fear of the unknown (Carleton 2016). This uncertainty intolerance exists on a continuum: our position on this spectrum affects how we react to daily life events. You may not respond to an event in the same way as I would or your friend would because, as we will see later, we filter our reality through our individual thinking, values and beliefs. The more intolerant we are about uncertainty, the more stressed and anxious we are likely to be. We are also more likely to overthink things and to start thinking negatively about the situation. Hebert and Dugas (2019) state that uncertainty intolerance is an increased risk factor for the development of Generalized

Anxiety Disorder (GAD), and that the best way for us to remove this fear of uncertainty is to learn that uncertainty is not dangerous for us. They indicate that 'there is no magic bullet and that it's all about putting ourselves in a situation where we can learn that uncertainty isn't dangerous' because 'over time this leads to a decrease in anxiety' (p.431).

Factors of influence on mental health – biological (genetics) and environmental (epigenetics), cultural and social

The emerging area of epigenetics could help provide a link between biological and other causes of mental illness. Epigenetics research examines the ways in which environmental factors change the way genes express themselves.

Dr Bruce Lipton, author of *The Biology of Belief* and a stem cell biologist, explains that at the beginning of his career as a researcher he was teaching genetic determinism, which holds that genes are not only capable of turning themselves on and off but also regulate our physical structure and our emotions and behaviours; this is all hereditary. The idea was that 'these are your genes; this is your life'. But through his work on stem cells, he discovered that our genes are controlled by the environment, and more specifically by our perception of the environment. This allows dynamic control of your biology.[26] Again, this research is really important when we reflect on how we think or talk about mental health. Lipton's work is really freeing too. I don't know about you but when I discovered this, I felt liberated. What we were previously told: 'my fate is determined by genes and by what I was given at birth' is not true. Our thinking and environment can and do influence the activation or non-activation of genes. How cool is that!

The good news – neuroplasticity – our capacity for change

The Oxford Dictionary defines neuroplasticity as: 'The ability of the brain to form and reorganize synaptic connections, especially in response to learning or experience or following injury.' Our brain is not a complex machine and is not hard-wired and stuck the way it is. It is constantly being changed by experience. You will realize that your behaviours and thoughts are not the same today as they were ten years ago. These changes are possible because of neuroplasticity, which means that the brain changes its structure and organization through learning, experiences and adaptation.

Our brain is malleable; neuroplasticity is the 'muscle building part' of the brain. So the more you practise a thought or an emotion, the more you reinforce the neural pathway. But if you have a new thought, you create a new neural pathway and a new way of thinking or doing things. Every time you do something and repeat it over and over again, this leads to changes in how your brain works. This new neural pathway will become stronger. The skills you don't use fade away.

Remember – every time you think a thought or act in a certain way, over and over again, it strengthens it. Over time, that way of thinking or that action becomes automatic. You can rewire your beliefs and actions because of what you think or what you do. Neuroplasticity happens throughout life. Connections within the brain are constantly strengthened or weakened, depending on what is being used.

But the good news is that we are not fixed in how we think, learn and perceive, and we can change. I would highly recommend watching the video created by the company Sentis on neuroplasticity[27] as well as the documentary directed by Mike Sheerin entitled *The Brain That Changes Itself*.[28]

The work carried out at King's College London and mentioned in the previous section clearly demonstrates that through neuroscience we can understand the neurochemical response that happens in our brains and bodies because of exposure to stress and challenges. These responses are there for all humans, but vary depending on who we are as individuals.

What does this mean for the Higher Education sector?

In the last decade, the concept that all aspects of our life should be happy and stress free has appeared. I am trained in Mindfulness, Neuro-Linguistic Programming (NLP) and hypnotherapy so I do not disagree with the notion of 'happiness in life', far from it. In fact, I believe that there is a real need for more skills to enhance our well-being: for better relationships, more engagement, more purpose and meaning in our lives (more on this in Part III). The issue with the notion that everything in our life (at school, university, work) should go smoothly and without a 'glitch' is that it conveys the idea that everything we encounter in our daily experience is supposed to be stress free.

It is important to realize that if we do not teach or encourage young people to solve problems using positive methods that lead to good outcomes, then they are going to turn to negative methods that lead to bad outcomes. This is part of the challenge currently facing Western societies. In NLP, there is a presupposition which says that 'behind every behaviour is a positive intention'. This means that every time we do something, it is usually done because we believe it will help us to 'achieve something' or to 'get away from a painful situation'. This is why, for example, young people start self-harming as a way to cope with their intense emotions or students drink a bottle of wine every night. They have found an 'unresourceful state' to cope with their emotions.

If we buy into the notion that normal life is pathology (i.e. that it's conducive to illness or disease), we start looking for ways to 'no longer be stressed'. We look for the next 'thing' that will provide us relief or pleasure. But that does not make sense because the stress response, which is in every single one of us, is the phenomenon that drives adaptation and resilience in life. We wouldn't be here as human beings without this faculty as our ancestors would not have survived.

We all experience difficulties in life. There are some things that provide a challenge, which is a necessary part of being a human being; the way we frame it can enable or disable us. Take for instance some of the students I interviewed, who were told by their doctors: 'this is going to be a lifelong problem, you can't improve'. Yet there are all kinds of evidence that given time they will recover. I think this notion that somehow you can't live with and recover from certain mental illnesses or disorders is very disabling.

Important final points to consider

We are not fragile little eggs like Humpty Dumpty, which will fall and break. We are resilient beings, far more than we even know. We have managed to evolve and grow in different environments throughout history. It is important to remind young people of this.

In his book *Antifragile – Things That Gain from Disorder*, Nassem Taleb shared a spectrum in response to stress – randomness, uncertainty errors and most importantly time

– with fragile at one end, robust in the middle and antifragile at the other end.[29] He says that the fragile breaks when faced with challenges, the robust doesn't care too much and the antifragile becomes stronger. Dr Paige Williams has tapped into Taleb's work and researched this concept of 'antifragile' further as a way to move beyond resilience. She has written a book called *Becoming AntiFragile: Learning to Thrive Through Disruption, Challenge and Change* and has created an antifragile survey. Her work demonstrates how to improve from challenging experiences, confirming that it is indeed possible to flourish despite struggles.

The next sections of this book will aim at introducing specific tools for students and tutors to take action on their journey to flourishing.

PART II

THE IMPLICATIONS FOR EDUCATION

Chapter 3

Time for a new model?

*'Education is the most powerful weapon by which you
can change the world'*
– Nelson Mandela

Cognitive, emotional, physical, social, spiritual health – always kept separate

In Western societies, we are taught to look at our thoughts, emotions, bodies and interactions separately from each another. We seem to keep them completely independent and compartmentalized. But what if they were in fact not separate but intertwined? Could our mental health have an impact on our physical health or our physical health have an impact on our emotional, social and mental health?

Some specialists also seem to agree with this idea. In her 2015 article entitled 'The nervous system and resilience',[30] Leitch states that the term 'mental health' is outmoded. She adds: 'We know that the mind and body are a system, inseparably connected; so we really need a term that reflects interventions that explicitly work with both' (p.1). Pert (1999) described this as 'body-mind'. Others use 'holistic' or 'integrative' models. The fact that there is no universally used and understood term reflects the fact that this is a relatively new frontier for psychotherapists and other clinicians and practitioners. The importance of our gut microbiota, has become a focus of research, particularly for those interested in the brain and behaviour. For example, according to Dinan and Cryan (2015), gut microbiota has recently been profiled in relation to a variety of conditions, including autism, major depression and Parkinson's disease.

What if they are all a 'continuum'? Corey Keyes's model as an exemplar

Prior to the progress made by modern medicine, we would consider someone to be physically healthy if they were not stricken by an illness. Nowadays, all the progress and technology has changed our definition of physical health. It ranges from total fitness to being unfit (due to several aspects such as no physical activity; nutrients and diet; drugs, cigarettes and alcohol consumption; self-care, for example, looking after oneself when we suffer from a cold; rest and sleep). But when we are physically unfit, it doesn't mean that we are suffering from an illness. Of course, the longer we carry on our unhealthy habits, the more likely it is that we will develop medical conditions such as high cholesterol, cancer or diabetes.

What if the same applied to cognitive, emotional, physical, social and spiritual health?

The mental health continuum: from languishing to flourishing in life

As we have previously seen, mental health is a 'state of well-being'. Keyes (2002) describes it as a 'syndrome of symptoms of positive feelings and positive functioning in life' (p.46). He reviewed and conceived of dimensions and scales of subjective well-being as mental health symptoms.

A diagnosis of the presence of mental health is described as flourishing, and the absence of mental health is characterized as languishing.

When reflecting on Keyes' concept, we realize that it is possible to have either high mental health (or flourishing) or low mental health (or languishing). We can go up and down the continuum depending on various factors but this does not mean that we have a mental illness or disorder. In fact, it is actually possible to be diagnosed with high mental illness or disorder but to be flourishing at the same time and to be able, as WHO (2004) states, to 'realize our own potential, cope with the normal stresses of life, work productively and fruitfully, and be able to make a contribution to our community' (p.1). The stories shared by the students I interviewed certainly support this idea.

It is also possible to be languishing and have a mental illness or to be flourishing with low mental illness or no mental illness, and finally to be languishing with low or no mental illness.

According to Keyes, mental health is more than the presence and absence of emotional states. Emotional well-being is a cluster of symptoms reflecting the presence or absence of positive feelings about life. Symptoms of emotional well-being are ascertained from individuals' responses to structured scales measuring the presence of positive affect (e.g. an individual is in good spirits), the absence of negative affect (e.g. an individual is not feeling hopeless) and perceived satisfaction with life.

People with mental disorders want to be accepted and to be accepting of others and themselves, to contribute and belong, to express their ideas and opinions. They are not different from anyone else. Keyes argues that his idea can be applied literally to everybody, regardless of whether they are suffering with a mental disorder. For him, illness is simply a small part of what constitutes us and what we must deal with to face this task of trying to flourish.

What is a flourishing student versus a languishing individual?

In his chapter, 'Complete mental health: An agenda for the 21st century', Keyes (2003) defines languishing as a state where the individual is devoid of positive emotion towards life, is not functioning well psychologically or socially, and has not been depressed in the past year.

He also states that complete mental health includes three clusters (emotional, psychological and social well-being) and provides a clear definition of the 14 potential qualities a flourishing individual would have (p.299).

Positive feelings: emotional well-being, which includes:

Positive affect: the person is regularly cheerful, in good spirits, happy, calm and peaceful, satisfied and full of life.

Happiness: the individual feels happiness towards the past or about their present life overall or in domains of life.

Life satisfaction: sense of contentment or satisfaction with past or present life overall.

Positive functioning: psychological well-being and social well-being:

Self-acceptance: positive attitude towards oneself and past life, and concedes and accepts varied aspects of self.

Personal growth: insight into one's potential, sense of development and open to challenging new experiences.

Purpose in life: has goals, beliefs that affirm sense of direction in life and feels life has purpose and meaning.

Environmental mastery: has the capability to manage a complex environment and can choose or create suitable environs.

Autonomy: comfortable with self-direction, has internal standards, resists unsavoury social pressures.

Positive relations with others: has warm, satisfying, trusting relationships and is capable of empathy and intimacy.

Social acceptance: positive attitude towards others, acknowledging and accepting people's complexity.

Social actualization: cares and believes that, collectively, people have potential and society can evolve positively.

Social contribution: feels that one's life is useful to society and that one's contributions are valued by others.

Social coherence: has interest in society, feels it's intelligible, somewhat logical, predictable and meaningful.

Social integration: feels part of, and a sense of belonging to, a community, derives comfort and support from community.

When I interviewed Dr Keyes, he told me that in his work he mirrored what the psychiatrists used to do to diagnose depression; and that for him, in essence, good mental health is flipping depression on its head, or looking at the other side of the coin. To diagnose positive mental health, just like psychiatry is required for depression, you need at least one sign of emotional well-being every day or almost every day, for two weeks or more. This is combined with at least 6 out of the 11 signs of functioning well, which can be either psychological well-being, social well-being or some combination, and again, every day or almost every day. In short, you only need 7 out of the 14 signs of flourishing to have good mental health. He also mentioned the idea that perhaps because of these combinations there are different topologies of flourishing, such as purpose in life and contribution, a person's autonomy, mastery and interest in life. Depending on the individual, the combinations will change.

At this point I would like to mention another point Keyes made when we chatted. We have a tendency to look at the extremes – we talk about flourishing or languishing or mental health or mental illness but a large proportion of us are in the middle, neither languishing nor flourishing with a potential to tip into either category. When we are languishing, our potential to tip into mental ill-health skyrockets. It is vital to not overlook nor underestimate this population if we want to make a difference. With more mental health literacy and a greater understanding of how to promote good mental health, we have more of a chance to reduce the risks of developing depression and anxiety.

The World Health Organization's definition of health and link with the new concept of 'flourishing student'

If mental health does not simply equate to a lack of mental illness but to a whole state on its own, 'a state of well-being' or 'flourishing' – how would you react to the following sentence: 'there is a state of well-being or flourishing crisis among students'? How about 'a state of well-being problem or issue'?

You would probably think that as a French native speaker, my knowledge of English is not very accurate or fluent; yet, to some extent we all seem to use the same collocations with the word 'mental health' without even questioning it.

Therefore, I would argue that it would be far more beneficial to ask why some students struggle to accomplish this state of well-being which would enable them to realize their own potential and cope with the normal stresses of life, work productively and fruitfully, and most importantly contribute to their community.

So, is it time to review this paradigm to focus on well-being and health based on a balance between cognitive, emotional, physical, spiritual and social health and not as separate entities? The positive dimension of mental health is stressed in the World Health Organization's definition of health contained in its constitution: 'Health is a state of complete physical, mental and social well-being and not merely the absence of disease or infirmity' (WHO 2005, p.100).

In 1969, Boucher and Osgood published a paper entitled 'The Pollyanna hypothesis' in the *Journal of Verbal Learning and Verbal Behavior*, in which they concluded that 'humans tend to look on (and talk about) the bright side of life' (p.1). Jing-Schmidt (2007) argues that we create and use more good words not, as Bierwisch (1967) suggests, because of people's tendency to consider the good as the normal state of life and the bad as the abnormal but in the hope that we can verbally construct a safer world for ourselves, precisely because the good cannot be taken for granted in the real world.

I cannot help but wonder if using this 'Pollyanna hypothesis' or 'positive bias' instead of 'negative bias' in current language around 'mental health' would help us construct a 'safer world' for ourselves and our students. If so, what positive words might we want to use? 'State of well-being' and/ or 'flourishing'?

Chapter 4

A new model based on students' stories

*'You never change things by fighting the existing
reality. To change something, build a new model that
makes the existing model obsolete'*
– R. Buckminster Fuller

Some of the students I interviewed reported that when they arrived at university, they regularly felt lost and lonely. This is quite normal since they have lost their connections and left their support network back home. They used to go to a secondary school where they were told that they were A* students, that they were amazing and that they could do and achieve anything they wanted. Their teachers really supported them and helped them organize their workload and plan their essays by looking at their plans, drafts and by making regular suggestions. Teachers also designed lessons around them and their preferences. They lived at home and their parents did a lot for them. Then suddenly, they arrive in a new city, they are put in halls of residence and asked to make new friends and get on with their academic work at university, which is so different from what they are used to. This could be described as the 'big fish in a small pond' syndrome.

Students reported experiencing not only social but also cultural isolation, which leads to a real culture shock. We normally associate culture shock with experiences in a foreign country or abroad but Oberg's (1960) early definition was: 'Culture shock is precipitated by the anxiety that results from losing all our familiar signs and symbols of social intercourse' (p. 177). P. Adler's (1975) definition of culture shock is psychologically more descriptive and explanatory:

> Culture shock is primarily a set of emotional reactions to the loss of perceptual reinforcements from one's own culture, to new cultural stimuli which have little or no meaning, and to the misunderstanding of new and diverse experiences. It may encompass feelings of helplessness, irritability, and fears of being cheated, contaminated, injured or disregarded. (p.13)

Another commonality in the students I interviewed was the fact that many of the students suddenly experienced what they described as 'life difficulties'; for some of them it was the first time they had gone through such difficulties since things always *went smoothly before then*'. One student described it by saying:

> *My dad had an affair in my second year – a few family members close to me died in my first and second year. When I got back from my year abroad my boyfriend of three years split up with me. I had planned to move in with him and I had to move in with random people. My drink got spiked and I ended up in hospital at the beginning of my final year.*

To me, the culture shock makes so much sense. Even if they are British and have been raised in the British system, the new system they must adjust to at university feels like a completely foreign environment. I often joke to students that learning academic writing is a bit like learning a foreign language. The way British universities function, as well as the new approach to learning and teaching with lectures and seminars for example, will all seem unfamiliar. One student I interviewed told me:

> *When I first arrived I was very happy and the first week was fun and I went out a lot. And then, it hit me! I had a lot of work to do and I had to become much more independent in my way of working. Much more than I'd ever had to at school. And boy did I struggle with this. There were also all these new words such as 'independent thinking' and 'critical thinking'. None of these made sense and I wasn't always comfortable asking what it meant.*

At university, many academics and lecturers expect students to deepen their knowledge and understanding of a specific subject and to develop different skills. This can also generate a lot of stress, particularly if a student has got used to navigating the schooling system and has become good at playing the game – learn by heart and regurgitate. Another student alluded to this when they told me: '*I wanted my tutor to tell me exactly how to write the essay and what to put in it but I was told that I had to read and to decide for myself. That was a very stressful, frustrating and scary experience.*'

Many of the students I spoke with told me how much they wished that they had asked for help immediately at university rather than letting the problems build up. They also wished they had tried finding coping mechanisms and discovered what worked best for them as individuals. We could compare this ability to identify new sources of support in a new environment with how the roots of a plant or flower must react to its environment. In a 2013 article titled 'The intelligent plant', Pollan explains that scientists have found that the tips of plant roots, in addition to sensing gravity, moisture, light, pressure and hardness, can also sense volume, nitrogen, phosphorus, salt, various toxins, microbes and chemical signals from neighbouring plants.[31] Roots about to encounter an impenetrable obstacle or a toxic substance change course before they make contact with it. Roots can tell whether nearby roots are self or other and, if other, kin or stranger.

So, where do we start?

The Flourishing Model (FM)

As I researched this book and came across the concept of flourishing, it immediately made me think of a flower and I decided to use the notion of a flower as an analogy to represent the student and their experience upon arrival at university. This is when the Flourishing Model came to life. What's interesting about this model is that it is not a 'one size fits all'. Through the 23 interviews I carried out, I saw that students' coping strategies for aspects in each part of the model may slightly differ. Overall, however, it is clear that this model can be a good guiding principle to lead a more flourishing life and to identify which areas might need to be improved and developed. You might want to explore this with your tutees or for yourself.

Our bodies are 'ecosystems' with trillions of cells collab-
orating together. We need to understand who we are as individuals: what works for us and what doesn't work in terms of
stress and well-being. As babies, and to some extent as young
children before we were conditioned and experienced incul-
turation (where we learnt and adopted the norms, beliefs and
values of the culture we grow up in), we listened to our inner
guidance much more. We told our parents when we were
hungry or had enough, for example. I'd like you to pause and
think about this aspect. Do you as an adult feel that you know
yourself well enough? What about your students and tutees? If
I am honest, I feel that it has taken me years (as I aged) to really
discover who I am as an individual and to be able to show up
more authentically. And I feel it's an ongoing process that starts
at birth and ends when we die – from cradle to grave.

This metaphor of the flower suggests that it is a continuum
and an ever-changing state that fluctuates for the flower, each of
its petals, moment to moment, day by day. The flower will open
or close depending on how each of its components is doing.

If you look in nature and observe flowers, you will see
that to be in full bloom, a flower needs to be totally open
with all its petals wide. You will also notice that all flowers
are different. In spring, rows and rows of daffodils appear on
the side of the road; some are taller, smaller, yellower, whiter,
more orange than others. They aren't looking around asking
themselves and others 'why am I taller than you?' or 'why
are you bigger/yellower than me?' They simply are. They
are firmly rooted in the soil, simply being themselves in the
present moment, in the now. This is the notion I would like
to encourage with this metaphor.

So let's imagine that our organization or institution is a
garden or an ecosystem and that everybody is a flower or

a flowering plant. We are all different types of flower. We can be daffodils, sunflowers, ivy or water lilies. All of us contribute to the diversity of that ecosystem; we form an ecosystem that is part of a bigger system. This means that we have completely different needs and all look different too. This is true of us as individuals. We are all unique individuals with different bodies and body shapes, strengths, weaknesses and with different interests and passions. It is therefore important that each one of us, staff and students, understand and know who we are as individuals. What part of the ecosystem are we and how do we contribute to it? How does it affect us too? This is particularly useful to remember in the context of education as some students tend to see how well or badly they do in comparison to others. This *comparatitis* – the need to constantly compare oneself to others negatively – is having a negative impact on young people. It is compounded by social media and highlight reels which make them believe that everybody is having a fantastic time (and they are not). They forget that their friends might have been upset or facing a challenge a few hours before but they never posted about it. If the student accepts the fact that he or she may be a sunflower and that one of their peers might be a bluebell, they would not feel the need to compare themselves to others and would simply accept being the flower they are. They would understand that it is in fact pointless to compare themselves to others.

But we all have one thing in common: as mentioned at the end of Part I, we are not fragile; we are all resilient and can take care of our own needs and have real abilities to grow and thrive. One example is that as we grow up, we slowly learn to speak or to crawl and walk; even when we fall and hurt ourselves, we still get up and try over and over again. We don't simply 'give up' because this 'walking malarkey' is far too difficult.

It is also possible to accept that if you are an ivy, you are likely to be far more resilient and able to climb walls than if you are a sunflower or a poppy. This makes the concept of 'stress bucket' and vulnerability even more obvious. If, as a member of staff (acting as a member of the gardening team or caring for the flower), I treat you (the sunflower) in the same way as I treat the ivy and expect the same thing from you, then it isn't going to work. I cannot expect you to climb up a wall because you are more likely to spread than to climb. That's what you do best. So as a tutor, I am one of the gardeners in this university garden (I am one of the many people in this gardening team who are involved in tending to the students' needs, including other university staff but also friends, family and others outside the university environment). I will look at what you do best and will try and encourage you to grow as well as possible by providing you with all that you need as a sunflower.

Of course, this game of comparing ourselves started at a young age so it is not going to be easy to introduce change. In fact, I think it starts from the minute we start using language because we are taught what things are and what they mean. We then start comparing different objects with each other. Our parents, without even realizing, compare us to our siblings and that's when this game is introduced in our life and becomes habitual. But change is entirely possible, particularly if we accept this possibility ourselves and encourage our students to do the same.

The standardized system in English schools means that young people are not encouraged to discover what type of flower and plant they are or how they contribute within the ecosystem. They are told that they are all the same and that they all learn in the same way. I believe this strengthens the lack of self-understanding and self-awareness that we see in HE. If we believe we are like everyone else – an orchid or a daisy when we are a cactus – how is that going to work? We will try to behave like an orchid or a daisy when clearly we are neither. I truly believe that this analogy is extremely useful and important to understand. Our young people need to get to know themselves and to understand who they are as unique individuals. There is no single path but varied paths based on who they are as individuals and how they want to show up in the world. How do they want to contribute? What are their beliefs and values? What do they stand for? It's difficult to answer these questions if we don't know who we are as an individual, let alone show up authentically. We know that the teenage years are particularly difficult for young people as they experience changes in their bodies and the way they feel. Teenagers may want to become independent, but we also know that they want to belong and care about what others, particularly their peers and those who matter to them, think about them.

From my conversations with students, it is obvious that at secondary school, as flowers, students felt that they were surrounded by other flowers that were much more like them; many of them also felt that they were in a safe environment that provided them with all the nutrients, water, light, and so on, they needed. In fact, they were safe in their home garden too, surrounded by their friends and family. They had a real support network.

Going to university meant that they were uprooted from their 'comfortable patch' and put into a completely different soil. Based on what students said, it would seem that when they arrived at university these flowers were set into a specific soil that might not be best suited to them. We cannot plant all the flowers in the same soil and simply expect them to 'get on with it' in this new environment. And when we lose our psychological or emotional safety, we cannot flourish.

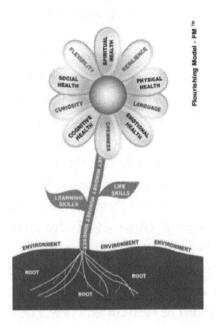

The university as a garden

I particularly like the metaphor of the university as a garden. The idea is to encourage every HE institution to recognize that it is like a garden that contains a huge variety of plants and flowers, which require different types of care to flourish. These flowers are all unique and individual but put together create a great composition that makes up the overall garden with different colours, shapes and fragrance. We don't want rows and rows of daisies or daffodils. For the garden to be truly beautiful, we need to have as much diversity as possible. When I discussed this with colleagues recently, one of them said that they saw themselves as "*the soil*" *or the environment in which others grow. At least, I have always felt more comfortable as a supporter, an enabler than a doer or achiever'*. I felt that was such a fantastic extension of the above metaphor. I hope you too will be inspired to find the time to creatively imagine what you would be in your own system.

Each university is an ecosystem of its own with each department or faculty a sub-section of that ecosystem. Like any ecosystem, each part contributes to its totality and makes up its beauty. It's important to spend time understanding each ecosystem and to shy away from suggesting 'one-size-fits-all' solutions. We will discuss this further in the last part of this book, but before we move on, it might be useful to mention Bronfenbrenner's theory of an 'ecological model of human development' (Rosa and Tudge 2013). In his 1975 work, he defined ecology as a fit between the individual and their environment, further adding that in order to develop, and not only survive, the fit between the individual and the environment must be even closer. We will be focusing on the individual and the Flourishing Model (FM) and its individual factors in this part of the book; however, a big oversight in the first edition of this book was suggesting that we only need to look after individuals' well-being without mentioning or considering the interactions within and between the different systems – I intend to remedy this in this second edition.

The environment

In the same way that a flower's growth is dependent on many factors, such as the amount of light, water and nutrients, so is our Flourishing Model (FM). The way our 'student flower' grows will depend on the environment, our gardening skills but also how well it absorbs the nutrients it is given. With proper care, the flower can grow and flourish in the soil that contains the right mixture.

If you look at the diagram, you will see that it consists of not simply the flower but also the environment. The idea is to represent the 'system' rather than simply an individual (as the flower) and 'the environment' as two different entities that have no impact on each other.

Many press articles often have a cause-and-effect way of presenting the issues experienced by students at university: 'Going to university stresses students out', but as this image shows, it is not as simple as that. The setting or environment has an impact on the flower but the flower also influences the system. All the people who are part of a HE institution system are not only part of the problem but also part of the solution. We all impact on the system: it is important that we all become aware of this.

The soil is therefore the environment – the way the flower opens or closes is co-dependent on the environment; it might 'flourish' much more in one environment than another. The blossoming of the flower also depends on how rich the soil is. As tutors, we form part of this environment, and I will discuss this interaction further in Part III. We can help our students flourish by providing them with the right 'nutrients' and 'food' they require. It may also depend on our 'gardening skills' and the care we provide our students. Students may for example respond to our own feelings of stress and anxiety.

We need to look at the model of the flower with the student being the full flower. As academics we need to view our students and their experience as a whole and not as fragmented. This means that we need to look at the environment and how we contribute to making this soil as rich and fertile as possible. For a plant to grow, it needs sun, water, nutrients and a good soil. So, with this metaphor – how is the soil in HE helping students to flourish? We need to make sure we realize that whilst we see our interactions with students as unique, students see their experience at university as a whole and each person is part of the bigger picture. We are all interconnected and impact on each other's experience. We need to take responsibility for our interaction with students and realize that they are different than their peers were ten years ago. The new generation has different needs, which we need to take into account. One of the students I interviewed said that she felt that her university tutors were the only adults she could talk to and confide in when she arrived, but sometimes she felt some tutors were not open and didn't really want to have a discussion with them. She also mentioned that she wouldn't want to discuss some of her personal issues with some tutors because they wouldn't understand or relate to her experience. I think it is extremely important for tutors to ask questions and to make sure that students feel welcome and that they become integrated within the university.

To go back to the analogy of the gardening team – if the gardeners trample all over the plants and flowers, how are they going to flourish and thrive? Similarly, if we keep pulling the plants out to check if they are growing (e.g. by over-assessing them), we can't then wonder why they are not growing as much as we would expect or like them to. As gardeners, we need to take good care of our flowers and plants. We need to care for and nurture each plant as a dynamic self-sustaining system with individual self-interests and needs, which is part of a bigger whole or community.

When we look at nature, a toxic environment clearly has an extremely detrimental effect on the plants and ecosystem. This is also true for us, and not just in terms of chemicals or other environmental toxins; it also applies to a toxic work or home environment where dysfunction and drama reign.

That said, although the environment has an impact on the flower and how well it is flourishing, students need to understand that they are not simply dependent on the care they receive from members of staff and academic tutors. They are also responsible for taking in the nutrients and taking care of themselves. A good gardener can give the plant all the nutrients and water it needs, but it will not flourish or look beautiful if it doesn't absorb any of it and transmit it across all its relevant parts. This is also true for our 'student flower'. They are responsible for the absorption of the information provided by tutors, for example.

When I use the word 'responsible', I refer to the concept of 'response ability', the ability to choose your response (as introduced by Jack Canfield in 2006) to external events. We are not victims of external events and can decide how to respond to an event that happens in our life.

As Senge explains in *The Fifth Discipline* (1990), it is also vital that students become aware of the 'enemy is out there' syndrome or what he describes as the 'propensity in each of us to find someone or something outside ourselves to blame when things go wrong' (p.8). In the last part of the book when we discuss the more systemic approach, I will mention the notion of holarchy coined by Koestler, which is the connection between holons. Just because we are individuals or holons which can act as an autonomous or self-reliant unit, let's remember that we are also part of a whole larger system and that the way we behave as individuals has an impact on the overall system. This is true for all of us, students and staff alike. Over the years, I have noticed a tendency in many of us (myself included) to be much more 'self-centred'. It's easy to explain this when we understand what fear and stress does to our nervous system. In short, when we are scared and in fear – living according to a fear-based approach – we feel that we need to protect ourselves against all the potential dangers out there and tend to become much more individualistic.

When things are difficult it is so easy to look at the external event and believe that it is happening TO us rather than FOR us. Blaming others and things may initially make us feel better but in the long term it is vital to get out of the victim mentality and mode of functioning and accept that as individuals we are responsible for the way we stand in the soil – how we take in the nutrients, the water, the sunlight that is being provided to us. We would not blame the sun when we are in the shade, for example; we would simply move. Students can take responsibility. Isn't it powerful to know that we can choose our reaction to an external event? I often say to my two boys that their names are not Pinocchio and that they don't have strings that people can pull to make them feel or do anything. They can choose and have a choice. They can choose their response to what is happening in their lives.

Why does this matter? In HE, so often I hear young people who say that because they are paying a lot of money for their education, they are entitled to more things, more help and more support. And whilst it is true that they deserve the best education possible and are entitled to attend classes that they love and will help them become the successful graduate, but most importantly the successful human being they want to become in their chosen field, I believe there is an issue around what universities are actually designed for. Is it to prepare students for life or to solely impart knowledge? Do we try to develop the whole student or just part? If we look at students holistically, academic tutors need to ensure that their environment, their soil, is as nutritive and empowering as possible so that they can grow and flourish. But it is also each individual student's responsibility to take on the nutrients and water and absorb them if they want to grow and flourish. We cannot do this for them.

It's the same if you have personal trainer sessions at the gym. He or she can show you how to do the exercises and what to eat to improve your level of fitness and lose weight. But your personal trainer cannot do the push-ups for you or the healthy eating or endurance training. This is also true of our relationship with students.

The idea here is not to induce guilt, which is a very unresourceful state. We do the best we can with the resources we have. There is no point in blaming oneself and feeling bad. The reality is that the most empowering step to take is to accept that regardless of what is currently happening in our life, ultimately we are the one who decides to either dwell on a feeling or thought or do something about it.

Flourishing students seem to take responsibility for the way they feel and think. They seem to know what they need more than anybody else because they are aware that they live with themselves 24/7. Nobody else does. They appear to do the best they can with the resources they have when things happen.

Flourishing students may realize that they can do better in a different 'environment'. For example, a student might not flourish as well in their halls of residence at the beginning of Year 1 as they do in their school or department or when they go back home because these are all different settings. The important point is to be aware of this and notice how individual flowers stand in the various environments and how they respond to them.

As I have mentioned before, we are not wooden puppets with strings that people on the outside can pull to make us feel or experience things. Yet we tend to use language and vocabulary that suggests as such when we say: 'he made me sad' or 'he upset me'. I know it is not easy to accept at first, and of course I am not saying that some people's behaviour can't be irritating or frustrating, but I firmly believe that people can't make us feel or experience anything. We can choose our response and this is where our 'response ability' lies!

In the last part of this book, we will look further at the notion of 'individual' versus 'environmental' responsibility. So often when I give a talk or a lecture, I hear 'sort out my environment and I will be fine'. Or I am told 'it's about the individual's responsibility'. For me, it's not so 'black and white' – it might be more about different shades of grey.

Yes, we need individuals to take care of themselves and to absorb the nutrients provided in the environment, but we also need to make sure that the environment is conducive for well-being (and I'll explain later why that is). I would argue that it is not a simple question of 'one' or the 'other' but rather an AND. I often feel that as human beings we have a tendency to oversimplify things. It makes sense, I guess, as our thinking is a source of high energy consumption. It makes us feel tired. The truth is that we are not simple creatures living in a simple environment, and we also don't live in a vacuum. The people and environment around us affect us, just as we affect others in our environment (at home, with our friends and family). Bronfenbrenner's model is extremely helpful and gives great insights into this. He starts with the individual, or in the case of his work, the child (microsystem), whose development is a complex system of relationships affected by the five levels of their surrounding environment (settings of family and school also called the mesosystem), the exosystem (which is a set of connections such as the extended family or neighbourhood), followed by the macro system (or the broad social and cultural values, laws and customs), and finally the chronosystem or the changes of time.

It may be useful to bear this in mind when we meet our new first-year students or when we deal with our tutees (or our own children).

The roots

As mentioned before, the flower is firmly established in the soil through its roots. These are strong and hidden from view. They include past experiences and memories (good, bad or even traumatic ones), values and beliefs, the metaprograms or strategies we use to make decisions, and hereditary traits inherited from our ancestors. Each flower due to its uniqueness has its own unique roots. We cannot expect them to be the same for everyone. These roots will determine not only how we show up in the world or the environment but also how we view (and respond to) said environment.

Memories

These are all the individual and collective experiences that have an impact on our current perceptions. Our present behaviours are significantly influenced by our collections of memories. For example, if you burn yourself on a stove, you will remember not to touch it the next time.

Values

These are the things that are most important to us. Values are our next most unconscious filter and are based upon our experiences to date. Values are linked to our beliefs and influence what we consider to be right or wrong, good or bad. They are context specific; therefore, what is important in one area of your life may not be important in other areas.

Beliefs

Beliefs are what support our values. They are what we hold to be true about ourselves, others and the world. They are thoughts that we have had consistently over a long period. Whether religious or not, we all have beliefs, and their quality significantly influences our quality of life. Some of our beliefs are more empowering, whilst others tend to be more limiting (as we will see below in Exercise 2).

The metaprograms

This is a Neuro-Linguistic Programming (NLP) concept that enables us to get to the way we process information. Metaprograms are extremely important as they give us an indication of how people process information and data. If we pay attention to the language used by students (not just the content but the words), it is possible to discover some metaprogram preferences and how they can impact how we deal with situations. There are seven main metaprograms.

1. 'Big picture' or 'small picture': Do you need details before you can start seeing the big picture or do you

actually need a vision or a big picture before you can work on the details of a plan?

2. Towards or away from: This is all about your motivation. Do you tend to be motivated more by the end goal (towards) or by the idea of moving away from something negative (away from)? Again, if you are 'away from', relevant language will need to be used to motivate and energize you, which will differ from the vocabulary used by a 'towards' person.

3. Options or procedure: Do you prefer clear instructions and procedures so that you know what you are doing? Or do you prefer options and really enjoy it when things are flexible and can be changed or when you can improvise?

4. Internal or external: Do you make decisions based on your own internal criteria or yardstick or do you need external feedback and information to help you decide that you are doing the right thing or before making a decision?

5. Proactive or reactive: Do you tend to start something and get going straight away or do you wait until people start and then follow?

6. Match or mismatch: Do you tend to notice similarities first or do you notice differences? Do you prefer noticing when things are the same or how different things are?

7. Self or others: Do you tend to view things from the self and based on 'you' or do you see things from the point of view of others? If you want to influence a student who is focused on the 'self' it will be important to focus on the personal benefits they will gain.

It is important to remember that these metaprograms are not negative or positive; they just are and we use them in an unconscious way, which is why they are hidden in the roots. They will show up in our language (part of the petal) if we listen carefully, and in the language of others. Please also remember that they may change depending on the environment and that they are a blend, so may be different when you are with your family, friends, boss, playing a competitive game, and so on. Being curious and paying attention to our metaprograms as well as those of students is extremely useful: it enables us to use language that is more likely to influence and have an impact on the student and their experience at university.

Specific tools for the teacher:

Exercise 1 – Identify your values

A quick exercise to recognize and identify your values in life and what matters the most to you.

Let's see what is important to you in life: what your values are. They guide our every decision and satisfying or violating them can produce strong emotional reactions.

Now have a go:

The simplest way to discover your values is to ask yourself the following questions:

What is important to you about [topic]?
What do you want in/out of [topic]?
What would having [topic] do for you?
So, for example – what is important to you in life?
Answer: honesty, authenticity, integrity, connections, love, kindness.

Can you then rank them by order of priority or preference? Very often we fail to notice that when people do or say things we don't like it is because they are 'trampling all over' (as I call it) our values. Once we recognize this, it is easier to deal with the person or situation and to recognize that whilst this is important to us, others may not share our values or see them as extremely important. We learn to accept that it is not good or bad; it just is the way each human being values aspects of life.

You could ask a more general question about 'life' in general or focus on other areas like 'relationships', 'family', 'work', 'business', and so on. You can decide all the parameters yourself.

Exercise 2 – Identify your beliefs

A quick exercise to recognize and identify your beliefs and to see if they are empowering or limiting you.

Now have a go:

Think about some of the beliefs you hold about various topics (including yourself) and note them down below. For each belief that you have identified, decide if they are limiting or empowering. If they are limiting, what would be a better and more empowering belief?

For example, 'I believe that I can meet and connect with new people easily and effortlessly' (empowering belief) or 'I struggle to make new friends' (limiting belief).

Start by asking yourself the following question: What do I believe about [topic]? Answer: I believe I am… [fill the gap]

In Exercise 3, I will show you how to change these beliefs with a simple belief change exercise.

Belief	Limiting/Empowering
Example: I struggle to make new friends	Limiting

To download and access the PDF for these two exercises, please visit www.flourishingeducation.co.uk or get in touch with me via email.

Exercise 3 – Simple belief change

A belief is only a thought that we keep thinking; it can easily be changed by changing the way we think about something. If you don't believe me, think back to when you were a child and believed in the tooth fairy or Father Christmas. When you discovered that it was in fact your parents, you changed the way you thought about both and created a new belief – they don't exist. This is the same with any belief you may have. For example – 'I can't do this easily.'

John Seymour shared this powerful exercise with us on our NLP practitioner course.[32] I have used it since then and I hope you find it as powerful as I have.

Now have a go:

1. Identify a limiting belief and check that students are 100% happy to change it. If there is some incongruence, identify what is worrying them and turn it into a positive.

2. State the current belief in the present tense and write it down.
3. State it in 'used to believe' tense.
4. Get the student to imagine the old belief behind them in the distant past.
5. What would be more useful to believe instead?
6. Invite the student to think of two or three options and then get them to choose the best option for them.
7. Imagine this new belief is now completely true.
8. What will be the best thing about this new belief as it becomes increasingly true? Ask the student to imagine the new belief becoming true and how different they would feel.
9. Could this new belief cause any problems?
10. What will be the first thing you see, hear and feel as this starts to become true?

Belief	I 'used' to statement	Two or three options	What would be more useful to believe instead?	Imagine the new belief as completely true
Example: Change takes time	I used to believe that change takes time	I can take a small manageable step every day Change can happen quickly Change is easy and quick		

To download the PDF worksheets for these exercises, visit www.flourishingeducation.co.uk or get in touch with me via email.

The stem

The stem of the flower feeds from the roots and represents the 'mindset' – the set of attitudes we hold. For the stem to be strong, we need to have strong mindsets.

For example, our mindset affects whether we believe we can grow or if our tutor or teachers expect us to grow, how we define failure and success, and understand and receive feedback (Dr Dweck's (2007) growth mindset/fixed mindset). This will have an impact on our academic and life skills, which grow from the stem and are fed by the mindset, or stem.

But the new generation of students and learners also need to take responsibility for their own flower and their own whole experience. This means looking at their stem – the mindset – and being willing to embrace change and committed and engaged with the environment they find themselves in. It might mean having to learn new academic and life skills that they do not yet possess and, most importantly, embracing the five skills – language, resilience, flexibility, openness and curiosity – and looking after their five 'healths', which we will discuss later on.

One of them is based on the 'growth mindset' as opposed to the 'fixed mindset', which was discovered and highlighted by Carol Dweck. She explained that when students are told that they are clever or intelligent when they do an exercise, they are less likely to want to take on a new challenge than if they are told that they did a 'good job' or made 'a great effort' when they tried to perform a task. For students to be flourishing, they need to embrace the notion that they have a 'growth mindset', which means that their identity as a learner is not 'fixed' or 'set'. Several of the students I interviewed shared that in the past they were told that they are A* students and that they are bright and clever; however, they now felt that they were not clever and believed they didn't deserve to be at university because they realized that they were surrounded by other A* students who were as good as them, if not better. Suddenly they were with others who were better than them and they were not so sure about their identity anymore. The beauty of having a growth mindset is that we first recognize that we don't have an identity – we ARE NOT an A* student – but that we have (or don't have) skills, knowledge and understanding. If we don't have these things, it does not mean that we cannot acquire them, far from it. It just shows us that there are things we need to learn and we can start asking questions freely because we are not afraid of what others may think about us.

The same goes with the notion of failure – at least three students I interviewed explained how afraid they were of failing and this notion that failure was almost like annihilation. But what if failure did not exist? Thomas Edison, who created the light bulb, said that he found 100 ways of not making a light bulb. There is also a Japanese saying that goes like 'success is falling down seven times and getting up eight'. This means that every time we do not achieve something, we get feedback instead: this tells us where we stand in comparison to what we want to achieve and we can see how we can bridge the gap.

For example, if one of our tutees comes to see us with their first mark and they tell us that they are not happy, we can start by explaining this concept of 'there is no failure, only feedback; no errors/mistakes, only learning'. So many first-year students arrive at university and are used to the concept of As and A*s that they really struggle with the HE marking system – the concept of a first, a 2:1, 2:2, and so on.

The important thing for their toolbox is to understand what is expected of them – do they understand the essay question or what is asked of them for their assignment; have they looked at the marking criteria and understand how they are going to be marked and assessed – what specific parts of their essays will be assessed (structure, content, for example) – and are they clear about what makes the difference between a first and a 2:1? They can then try to structure their essay to meet these requirements.

Reassure students that the mark does not reflect how clever or able they are but simply how well they performed in their assignments and responded to the question asked. A 58 or 62 is not a failure. These marks simply provide the student with feedback, telling them where they are on the scale and what they need to do next time to bridge the gap between where they are and where they want to be – maybe moving to a low first or a high first. When we give feedback, it is important to provide students with that 'feedforward' so that if they haven't yet clearly understood that marks do not reflect their level of intelligence but their ability to apply their critical and analytical skills to a specific topic or subject, they now understand this.

Interestingly, I can relate to this concept and no doubt so can you, to some extent. In our lives, we all have dreaded receiving feedback from people because we see it as a reflection on us, on how good or not good we are at what we do. During the interviews for this book, a couple of students stated that they avoid reading feedback because they take it personally; their sense of achievement is bound up with a sense of self and they start to believe that it shows that they are not good enough to be studying at university.

This leads nicely on to the third topic in mindset, which is feedback – students often see feedback as criticism of things they 'did wrong'. But feedback on an essay gives students further information on the good parts and what they did very well, and the parts which need improving and how – for example, learning to quote others better or using secondary literature to 'back up' their arguments. Feedback is not used to back up the notion of 'intelligence and identity as a good student or good learner' but simply shows students where they can improve. Encouraging students to engage with feedback is therefore vital if students want to grow, develop and improve.

I highly recommend using sandwich feedback with a change in the language from good, better to best – so the first bit of bread is all about the good parts of the essay, what the student did well and achieved in their work; the better part gives the student the 'meaty' bit they expect with the word 'but', providing students with all the important aspects of the work they need to focus on to improve (or 'feedforward'); and we finish with the best part of the essay or coursework: what we love the most about it.

For me, feedback is a little bit like a sat nav. It's the little dot that locates you on the map and tells you where you stand on a scale (from first-class piece of work to third class) and how to bridge the gap between where you currently find yourself and where you want to go. It's nothing to be afraid of and enables us to change, improve and grow so as to be welcomed and accepted. Even if I do admit that sometimes it is not easy to get feedback, particularly if it is presented in a 'harsh' way.

Specific tools for the teacher:

Exercise 1

Ask students for their definition of failure and success. Ask yourself how you would define failure and success. Is it the same? Different?

If working in groups, spend some time discussing these similarities and differences and decide on a common definition of 'failure' and 'success' that everyone is satisfied with.

Exercise 2

Ask students to define what 'growth mindset' and 'fixed mindset' are. Discuss these definitions and decide on a final definition they can remember and use on a daily basis.

I was told that in Papua New Guinea they say: 'Knowledge is only a rumor until it is in the muscle.' I think this is perfect to illustrate my point. Remind your students that just because something is understood intellectually, it doesn't mean that it is a lived experience.

Exercise 3

How do they receive feedback?

Ask your students how they view feedback. Very often students see feedback as a form of criticism or as a way of pointing out what they have done badly or incorrectly. Flourishing students seem to engage with feedback as they see it as a way of understanding what they can do differently next time and what they can improve. As with Exercises 1 and 2, encourage open discussion and conversations around the fear that receiving feedback generates for students. It is also an opportunity to discuss the fact that the mark is not the 'be all and end all'; in fact, feedback will enable them to gain a better grade next time.

Questions: How do you define feedback? How do you feel when you receive feedback? What do you do when you get an assignment back? Do you tend to look at the feedback or simply the mark? Why?

Exercise 4

Get students to challenge their beliefs around these concepts (you could use the previous exercises on identifying beliefs about feedback) and ask them what their reaction would be to this sentence:

There are no mistakes, only learning – no failure, only feedback.

When each of my boys started primary school and went to reception, I bought them a nice pencil and a rubber and told them that it was their best friend because every time they use the rubber to erase a mistake, they have learned something. They are now in Years 2 and 4, respectively, and I can confirm that they are not afraid of making mistakes. What would happen if we gave students a pencil and rubber when they start university and if we introduced these concepts to make sure that the 'stem' of their flower is strong and can lead to the acquisition of new academic and life skills they will need as part of their new environment?

Life and learning skills

Life and learning skills are closely linked and impact on the results students get at university greatly.

'If you don't know where you are going, you might
wind up someplace else' – Yogi Berra

Life and learning skills provide students with three main outcomes: effective learning, effective living and employability. It involves setting well-formed outcomes or goals and, using their summarizing and memorizing skills, students develop an understanding of the challenges required to adapt to student life, manage personal stress effectively, conflicts and relationships with family and friends, and most importantly to problem solve.

Learning skills

Learning skills involve all the tasks and activities required for learning: time management, note taking, study skills as well as action planning, goal setting and chunking down to take back control. When students are overwhelmed by the amount of work they have been set and the essays they have to write, I often suggest that they use the 'chunking down' technique.

Chunking down means looking at a task and cutting it into smaller parts that can be subdivided and clarified to help with the workload.

Action planning

Learning skills are not just about knowledge acquisition and are closely linked to the life skills young people require for the 21st century. Given that the current schooling system seems to focus more on the acquisition of this knowledge, it is even more vital that at HE level we ensure that young people develop and acquire all the skills they will need for their future as global citizens.

Action planning helps students to concentrate on their different ideas and decide on the steps needed to achieve their specific goals. It involves forming a one-line sentence or statement that clearly defines what they want to get done over a specific length of time. It enables students to achieve their objectives in life and to start planning for their future rather than being worried about it. Students can use lists in order, for example, to meet a deadline or to cope with the pressure of juggling various tasks.

Of course, this is not new for students: children learn to do this task from primary school and in particular in secondary school when their teachers ask them to note the Learning Objective or the WALT (we are learning to...) for each lesson. The idea is to encourage students to do this by themselves, independently and spontaneously, so that they can identify what they have learned or achieved either in a week or every day, for example.

I often recommend using a journal to do this on a daily basis. The journal can be used to record and write the various objectives and to keep track of progress but can also be used to review stressful events. Researchers Philip Ullrich and Susan Lutgendorf explored the effects of journaling on stressful events (2002). They found that students who focused on cognition and emotions developed greater awareness of the positive bene-fits of the stressful event than the other two control groups. A recent article in the New York Times described journaling as the cheapest effective act of self-care.[33] Dr Pennebaker, an American professor, has also discovered that expressive writing and jour-naling have an extremely positive outcome. When we journal, Dr Pennebaker says, it helps us organize events in our mind and most importantly make sense of it. Using some of the exercises below in a journal can help you and your students.

Identifying key issues and key outcomes

Issues can be defined as what we find problematic in our lives. They may involve people, emotions, money, work, tasks or family. I believe that issues can be very positive and can help us grow. We can learn a lot from the issues we encounter in life and can develop new skills or create new outcomes.

Positive psychology corroborates this with the concept of post-traumatic growth (PTG). Haidt (2006, p.135) cites Nietzsche's quote 'What doesn't kill you makes you stronger.' He also addresses the notion that stress and trauma can be good for people. He goes on to state that PTG directly contrasts with post-traumatic stress disorder, where individuals derive no benefit from their trauma, only pain and anxiety.

Previously, psychology tended to see stress and anxiety as negative and causing problems; however, recent research on traumatic events ranging from divorce to death and natural disasters or terrorist attacks (Haidt 2006) shows that even though the causes of PTG are vast, the benefits reported fall into three main categories.

- The individual feels stronger and finds hidden abilities and strengths. It changes the person's self-concept and gives them the confidence to face their challenges. For example, the positive belief that things happen not to us but FOR us and to serve our further development.
- The individual strengthens their relationships.
- The individual changes their priorities and philosophies concerning the present and the now and others (Haidt 2006; Shaw et al. 2005).

When I interviewed students who had experienced traumatic or difficult events, those who felt that they had recovered from the situation clearly reported that they thought they had grown emotionally, developing closer relationships with family and friends when they started discussing and sharing their issues. They now looked at life from a different perspective and considered their issues as 'less important'.

It is therefore important to be able to identify what some of our issues are in life. Initially, it is probably best to start with the smaller ones but as students build competence at dealing with their issues, they can start exploring more important ones. It is important to start slowly and to be gentle on oneself but also to have both issues and outcomes in our life plan.

The ability to set outcomes is something we need to learn as it is not innate. Defining outcomes will enable students to define what works best for them.

It is important to be aware of the beliefs and thoughts held about setting outcomes. If students feel that it is going to be hard work and difficult, then chances are it will be. As Henry Ford said, 'whether you think you can or you can't – you're right'. Seeing outcomes as a skill that can help them achieve more will be very beneficial for students.

From the main outcomes students set, they can draw daily outcomes that will enable them to take the steps towards successful completion of the outcomes. It is a good idea to encourage students to set daily outcomes through journaling: this will give them a sense of taking back control and being back in charge of their lives. When practised daily, this will become a habit and will make a big difference to the way they organize their daily activities and plan for the future.

Specific tools for the teacher:

Well-formed issues and well-formed outcomes

This activity will help you and your students to identify key issues and set key outcomes. This is a skill that I learned when I trained with John Seymour. We can develop it and learn through regular practice so that it becomes a daily and unconscious habit for success. Identifying key outcomes enables us to gain the best benefits in each area of our life we have chosen and identified. We identify two or three options and can then pick the best.

Now have a go:

Identifying a well-formed issue or problem:

Sometimes we are much better at expressing what we don't want to happen or to get than what we would rather have. A well-formed issue is likely to involve emotions.

Start with the following question:

What problem or issue are you currently experiencing? Just state it in the negative:

For example, I don't want to fail my exam because I will feel awful and not good enough.

To identify a well-formed outcome, ask yourself or your student: what would you rather have instead?

State in the positive: I want to pass my exam and feel good.

Check that you really want this – If I could pass my exam and feel good – would I take it? Would I be happy with that?

If yes, then continue. If no, then ask what is worrying you about this?

For example, I am not sure I can do this. Changed statement: I want to believe I can pass my exam and feel good.

Specific information: If I had a magic wand and could give you this right now, describe what would be happening?

Followed by: What would you be seeing, hearing and feeling?

Finally, ask if this is within your control – is this something you can achieve yourself? You can only control your own behaviours. You cannot influence others' decisions, thoughts or attitudes so it is important to focus on what YOU can achieve.

If you don't have an issue to solve, you can then focus on what you would like to do over the next couple of months. You can do this by asking yourself the following question:

What do I wish to achieve next?

I want to…

(state the sentence in the positive) and then follow the steps for the well-formed outcome described above.

To download the PDF for this exercise, visit www.flourishingeducation.co.uk or get in touch with me via email.

Life skills

The World Health Organization (2003, p.1) defined life skills as 'abilities for adaptive and positive behaviour that enable individuals to deal effectively with the demands and challenges of everyday life'. Life skills prepare a student to live in an independent way within a society.

Life skills include specific skills such as:

- Job-related skills – writing a CV, time management, presentation skills, planning skills, teamwork.
- Everyday living skills – shopping, cooking, washing, managing one's finances, which are vital parts of independent living; problem solving, the ability to ask for help when required.
- Self-reflection and understanding, stress management, critical thinking.

Some of these skills may not be as developed in young people, which is something I certainly noticed when I rejoined the university after a nine-year break. What young people could do in 2005, their peers do not seem able to do as effectively today. Of course, it is important not to generalize that this is the case for all students but there is clearly a lesser ability to deal effectively with the demands and challenges of everyday life. As we saw in Part I, this could be explained as the consequences of 'overparenting' or 'helicopter parenting' and the fact that many schools are guiding students through their GCSEs and A levels step by step. It would be interesting to research this further to see how these factors impact on students and their flourishing abilities.

The head of the flower

The 'head' of our flower is composed of five 'health concepts' – cognitive health, emotional health, physical

health, spiritual health, social health and five 'skills' –
flexibility, openness, curiosity, resilience and language use.

Before we start looking at each 'health concept', let's
address the importance of moving through life on 'autopilot' and the negative impact it has on our well-being.

Life on 'autopilot'

The Urban Dictionary defines autopilot as: 'when you do
something without realizing what you're doing (usually
results in making a mistake)'.

Using the same analogy of driving on 'autopilot', have
you ever driven on a motorway, deep in thought, only to
realize how far you'd gone? Have you ever closed your front
door without thinking, only to go back to double check
because you can't remember doing it? Or have you ever
walked back home from university but forgotten to stop at
the shop when you wanted to?

This is what I mean by life on 'autopilot'. We are not
conscious or aware of our thinking, of what we do on a daily
basis. For example, we leave our keys and phone somewhere
without focusing on the location and we then spend five or
ten minutes looking for them in a frenzy.

People sometimes fail to notice salient unexpected
objects when their attention is otherwise occupied;
researchers such as Kreitz et al. (2015) describe this as inattentional blindness.

I would suggest watching this great video entitled 'The
Monkey Business Illusion' by Daniel J. Simons, which really
illustrates this point.[34]

A break from autopilot

A 2010 study, entitled 'A wandering mind is an unhappy mind', completed by two psychologists: Matthew A. Killingsworth and Daniel Gilbert from Harvard University, can be found in the journal *Science*. Through their research, the authors concluded that people spend 46.9% of their waking hours thinking about something other than what they are currently doing, and this mind-wandering makes them unhappy. In fact, in their work, Killingsworth and Gilbert argue that 'The ability to think about what is not happening is a cognitive achievement that comes at an emotional cost.'[35]

Learning to become more conscious of our thoughts, emotions and sensations and directing our attention to them may also make us more aware of the arousal of the sympathetic or parasympathetic nervous system.

Leitch (2015) believes that understanding key reasons for the way we feel, think and act as we do can decrease the tendency to pathologize symptoms as character flaws or weakness. According to her, this sensation-level self-awareness is the key to living an embodied life, being grounded in the present moment, and being able to restore nervous system regulation using the Social Resilience Model (SRM) skills.

Being more present also enables us to develop more self-awareness and to discover who we truly are as individuals. It helps us to go beyond automatic thinking and emotional reactions and most importantly beyond the protective personalities we have developed over the years whilst being socialized and conditioned in our societies. We can decide if we want to keep any of these mental constructs and models. In truth, the issue is not really with our mental models. It is that most of the time we are not aware of our thoughts nor are we aware that how we think and view the world shapes our reality. The map is not the territory, as we say in NLP. The mental maps or models we use are not the world itself. If it were, we would see the world and reality in exactly the same way. The beauty is that by bringing awareness we can break out of this potential mental and emotional prison.

Cognitive health

Our cognitive health is linked to our logic, thinking and understanding. Without cognitive health, we cannot survive. Thanks to our cognitive health, there is some continuity in our thinking and we can understand the world around us and others. We often fail to see how important our thoughts are to our success or failure and to what happens in our life. As mentioned before, because we are often on autopilot, we fail to observe our thoughts and mental chatter; we simply identify with the situation and the thought without challenging them and taking them for what they are – things that can be changed. The problem with thoughts is that if we keep thinking the same things repeatedly, they become beliefs. When we identify fully with a situation and believe it totally, it becomes difficult and almost impossible to change, whereas if we are aware and notice that it is our thinking that creates our views of a situation, we can adopt the notion that change is possible. David Bohm, quantum physicist, summarized this beautifully when he said: 'thought creates reality and then says I didn't do it' (1994, p.27). Dr Lipton, whom we mentioned previously, says that through his work he's seen that the chemistry put into the blood by the brain is a direct complement to the picture we hold in our mind. In other words, the mind's image is translated by the brain into chemistry, which then goes to the body to create a physical complement to the image in the mind (2017, p.45).[36]

Braden (2012, p.17) confirmed this when he stated:

> In the instant of our first breath, we are infused with the single greatest force in the universe—the power (of thought) to translate the possibilities of our minds into the reality of our world ... an awesome power and our knowing that we are never more than a thought away from our greatest love, deepest healing, and most profound miracles.

Corcoran et al. (2010) explain that Mindfulness meditation promotes metacognitive awareness, decreases rumination via disengagement from perseverative cognitive activities, and enhances attentional capacities through gains in working memory; these cognitive gains, in turn, contribute to effective emotion regulation strategies.

Evidence provided by Siegel (2007a) indicates that Mindfulness meditators develop the skill of self-observation that neurologically disengages automatic pathways created from prior learning and enables present moment input to be integrated in a new way.

Observing our thoughts is like taking a step aside and becoming an observer, a fly on the wall, and we can then see ourselves thinking. We do not try to run away from the flow of thoughts or to even stop them because this is virtually impossible. What happens is that we become aware of the thinking but we don't engage or listen to it.

In Zen, they use the metaphor of the waterfall. We are between the waterfall (the flow of our thoughts) and the rocks (our bodies). We shift slightly to observe our thinking. We are not under the flow of water (we have enough distance not to get caught up in them) but we are not far away either (we have enough presence to be aware).

We use our ability to reflect and to self-observe and simply learn to watch our thoughts go by without trying to suppress them, as this would be counter-productive. We don't go looking specifically for our thoughts but simply acknowledge or accept each one as it comes up and let it go.

Moore and Malinowski (2009) compared a group of experienced Mindfulness meditators with a control group who had no meditation experience on measures assessing their ability to focus attention and suppress distracting information. The meditation group had significantly better performance on all measures of attention and had higher self-reported Mindfulness. Mindfulness meditation practice and self-reported Mindfulness were correlated directly with cognitive flexibility and attentional functioning.

As we have seen in Part I, individuals are capable of coping with normal life stressors as well as the ability to work productively. Mental health is very much linked to the other petals; in fact, it is often the only aspect of 'health' that the press and media talk about. Our behaviours are influenced by our thoughts and emotions, which in turn affect our social interactions.

I am sure that whilst you have been reading this book, your mind will have gone wandering. It's not good nor bad. That's what we do. We may make inner comments on what is unfolding and I call this our 'mental chatter' and sometimes our 'negative self-talk'. When we practise Mindfulness and bring awareness into our daily life, we become much more aware and shine light on these thoughts.

Researchers at UCL who tracked mental health since the beginning of the first lockdown in the UK found that individuals' mental health has been affected not only by experiencing adversities such as financial difficulties, unemployment as well as infection with the virus, but also by worrying about these consequences.[37]

Specific tools for the teacher:

Exercise 1 – Mindful breathing – Quick one-minute exercise

Turn on the timer on your phone for one minute. Focus on your breath and count every out breath as follows: in… out: one, in… out: two until you reach ten without being distracted by a thought, emotion or sensation. If you get distracted, simply start again at one.

For an even more powerful effect, you can use the technique that my wonderful friend Treesje shared with me, which has been tested by Dr Andrew Huberman in his laboratory and is described as the fastest way to adjust stress levels. You can watch a short video on YouTube[38] but in short, it's based on physiological sighs, which were discovered in the 1930s: animals and humans use two short inhales and longer exhales with the inhales done through the nose and the exhales through the mouth.

How was this exercise? Useful?

Exercise 2 – Breathing meditation MP3

Everyone breathes and can use their breath as the focal point of their meditation. Most of the time, we breathe and are not aware of it. Breathing is regulated by our automatic nervous system and it is only when and if I ask you to become aware of your breath as you read this that you will. We tend to be too busy with our thoughts, emotions and activities to notice our breath.

This meditation on the breath will not only be dealing with the air coming in and out of the lungs; it will also enable us to become aware of the sensations of that breath as it enters and leaves our body.

This meditation is also extremely beneficial because it will enable you to stop distractions and make your mind clearer and more focused. Your breath becomes the anchor of the distracted ship of your mind. It keeps you firmly IN THE PRESENT/IN THE NOW. You do not rush to the past or to the future. It is the focus and you bring your attention back to your breath, over and over again. Very often when we are stressed or anxious, we tend to hold our breath or do very shallow breathing. It is important to take deep breaths to anchor ourselves in the present moment.

At first, your mind may seem to be very busy and you might even feel that it is becoming busier. You are becoming more aware of how busy your mind actually is. There will be a great temptation to follow all the thoughts that arise but you can bring your attention back to the breath by focusing on it single-pointedly. If you discover that your mind has wandered off and is following a thought, bring it back to the natural sensation of the breath, over and over again. Repeat this as many times as necessary until the mind focuses on the breath.

This meditation can be practised daily – either first thing in the morning or last thing at night and will become the bedrock of our practice.

However, it would be extremely useful to remember your breath throughout the day and to focus on it for a minute or so when you get into the car first thing in the morning, when you make a cup of tea, before sending an email… There are many opportunities to include this activity in our daily life.

When there is a storm, the sea or the ocean becomes rough. Sediment is being churned up and the water becomes murky but when the wind dies down the sediments settle and the water becomes clear. In the same way, when the breath calms down the constant flow of thoughts, our mind becomes clear and peaceful.

Exercise 3 – Mindfulness and meditation on thoughts MP3

The Buddha said 'your worst enemy cannot harm you as much as your unguarded thoughts'. This meditation will therefore get us to notice our thoughts without engaging with them so that we can become more attentive to our thoughts as they come and go, more comfortable with the idea of engaging with each thought or not and more attuned with oneself and others.

Now have a go:

Ensure that you have your feet flat on the floor or if you are doing this lying down that your back is straight, shoulders gently relaxed. Gently close your eyes. If you don't feel comfortable closing your eyes, just focus your gaze about one metre away from you – a gentle gaze. Start by listening to the sounds around you. Then focus – you are focused on what you can hear around you. We are not making up stories about these sounds. Simply notice, acknowledge and welcome them and then let them go and move to the following sound you can hear. If your mind has gone off on a tangent or you are being distracted by a thought, a sensation in your body or an emotion, simply become aware, notice, acknowledge the object of distraction and bring your attention back to the sounds. Do this over and over again. That's the practice.

Now bring your attention inwards. Notice where you feel the sensation of your breath the most in your body. The natural flow of your breath. Is it the rising and falling of your chest or abdomen or the slightly cooler air as it comes in through your nostrils and warmer air as you breathe out? It is your breath and your body so there is no right or wrong way of doing this. You know what works best for you. Now, simply focus your attention on your breath – this breath, not the last one nor the next one. The breath becomes the anchor of the distracted ship of our mind. Thoughts, sounds, sensations, emotions will try and hijack your meditation. This is completely normal. Just like with the sounds, you simply need to notice, acknowledge and let them go and bring your attention to the breath. You do this over and over again. I would recommend starting with a three- or five-minute meditation. If you are doing this by yourself, you can use a timer to let you know when the time is up. If you are finding that your mind is really busy, you can count each outbreath (as in Exercise 1).

You can download the MP3 by visiting our website.

Emotional health

The Mental Health Foundation has described emotional health as 'a positive state of well-being that enables the individual to be able to function in society and meet the demands of everyday life' (p.178) (Kadam and Kotate 2016). Emotional health is also the degree to which students feel emotionally secure and relaxed in everyday life. Do they know what flourishing emotional health looks and feels like?

Our emotions act as our guide. They lead us to make decisions and take actions or not. Students I interviewed referred to their emotions as their 'gut feeling' or 'sensations' they experienced and which sometimes might motivate or deter them from doing something.

From a young age, we are taught to control our emotions. For example, as a child if we are sad or hungry, or annoyed and we start crying, our parents tell us to stop. I believe emotions are meant to be felt and experienced. As Peter McWilliams (1994) stated, 'emotion is energy in motion'. It is meant to be experienced and then it disappears. Young children are again great examples of this: they might have a massive tantrum, roll themselves on the floor and then get up and start playing again.

As human beings, we need to start being with our emotions a lot more and to accept them. Very often, instead of acknowledging how they are feeling, students interviewed stated that they saw their emotions as embarrassing, wrong or something to be ashamed of. They often reported telling themselves that they 'are silly to feel this way' and that they often try to ignore the emotions, brush them under the carpet or push them away. I really like the analogy of a pressure cooker. If we keep pushing things down and down, at some point the pressure kept inside the pressure cooker will have to be let out and usually it explodes because we haven't used the 'release valve' to let some of the pressure out.

We also need to know a lot more about emotions. In her TED talk called 'You aren't at the mercy of your emotions – your brain creates them', Professor Lisa Feldman Barrett explains that the results of all her research are overwhelmingly consistent.[39] 'We are not born with emotional circuits in our brain. Emotions are "guesses" based on billions of brain cells working together in any given moment and we have more control than we think we do.' Our emotions are built. When an event happens, we ask ourselves 'what is this most like in my past experience?' So, our brain doesn't react to the world.

Using past experiences based on similar situations, our brain predicts and constructs our experience of the world. We make sense of the world and make meaning through predictions which are primal and enable us to do so in a quick and efficient way. Feldman Barrett says that as humans we can make feelings such as calmness, agitation, comfort or discomfort. These simple feelings are not emotions. They are simply telling us what is going on inside our body, like a barometer. That's where our brain comes in to give us more detail. Depending on the context, and through prediction, our brain links what is going inside us with what is going on around us in the outside world to know what to do next. We are not at the mercy of our emotion circuits, and we have more power than we think. Feldman Barrett calls this being the architect of our experience.

This can only be achieved by being present with what is currently happening in our lives rather than being on auto-pilot (as mentioned previously). Mindfulness, as we will see in the next section, can help us with this. Although very positive and empowering, this means more responsibility. Who is responsible? Who can change these predictions? We can. We can decide how we construct these sensations and become really good at challenging the predictions. We don't have to repeat the past says Feldman Barrett. When we are emotionally healthy, we tend to feel relaxed; our body is relaxed and not tensed, we are open to new experiences and new ideas. We have fewer automatic reactions as well as less anxiety and panic over events in our lives. It also means that we are likely to be calmer and more patient with ourselves and others.

As a result, we do not judge or criticize our emotions; we accept them for what they are and if we react to a situation, we do not judge or criticize ourselves or others. We recognize, as mentioned previously, that we do the best we can with the resources we have at the time; hindsight is fantastic but we didn't know how to deal with an event prior to this, otherwise we would have reacted differently. There is therefore no point to feel guilty about it all.

Several of the students I interviewed reported not feeling safe and secure in their own emotions and feelings and said that they tried to avoid or control their emotions most of the time. They also mentioned at times they felt that their interpersonal and public interactions with other individuals were affected by their own feelings and emotions. This in turn affected how 'open' or 'closed' they felt towards the person.

They also stated that they would like to learn to express their feelings in healthy, assertive ways and not to inhibit their emotions. The students admitted that there was a clear difference between a negative versus a positive attitude to life but that at times a certain feeling of lack of control led them to procrastinate and make ineffective decisions in their work and personal lives.

One skill that seems to help students become more aware of their emotions (and the wider range of emotions they experience throughout the day) and feelings is the practice of Mindfulness.

Specific tools for the teacher:

Mindfulness to become more aware and present

What is Mindfulness?

The Oxford Dictionary defines it as:

> A mental state achieved by focusing one's awareness on the present moment, whilst calmly acknowledging and accepting one's feelings, thoughts, and bodily sensations, used as a therapeutic technique.

Over the last 40 years, a lot of studies have researched and analysed the benefits of Mindfulness. Gunaratana (2002) explains that Mindfulness meditation has its roots in Zen and Buddhist meditation; for example, he tells us that Vipassana, a form of meditation that derives from Theravada Buddhism, is a Pali word for insight or clear awareness and is a practice designed to gradually develop Mindfulness or awareness. A secular practice was introduced by an American Doctor, Jon Kabat-Zinn, through his Mindfulness-Based Stress Reduction (MBSR) programme, which he launched at the University of Massachusetts Medical School in 1979.

Kabat-Zinn is considered as one of the founders of the Mindfulness research movement. For this reason, his definition of Mindfulness as 'paying attention in a particular way: on purpose, in the present moment, and nonjudgmentally' (1994, p.8) is one of the most recognized definitions of Mindfulness in the world.

It is particularly important and useful to see Mindfulness not simply as a tool but a way of life. This means that we stay focused in the present moment, in our bodies, with our emotions, able to observe our thoughts and to spot some recurring thoughts. Mindfulness also involves connecting to others, and practising compassion and loving kindness, which are so important for our social health.

I do not believe that being human requires us to be like monks and to constantly meditate. I also think that too much introspection can also be dangerous as it can make us focus too much on what is going on 'inside' and 'within' and to become slightly self-centred. We are social animals and as we will see later on with 'social health', it is important to also turn to the world and communicate with people if we want to flourish.

It is simply a question of using these great skills and to turn Mindfulness into something we do on a daily basis. We are present. We do not rush to the future constantly worrying about what is going to happen next and we do not revisit the past, feeling sad and nostalgic, sometimes wishing that we could change things we have done or said or change what people did or said to us.

It is all a question of balance. My intent with this book is to provide you with information about mental health but also help you gain direct awareness of what you are paying attention to, your language, behaviours, likes/dislikes/preferences and how you make sense of the world and give it personal meanings. I strongly believe that ideas are not set in stone and are context- and stress-related and so can be changed. This is true for all of us. The best way to do so is by gaining said awareness because once you become aware, it opens a spectrum of possibilities which change your view of the world. It's not 'this or that', 'stereotyping' or 'pigeonholing'. Instead, it is accepting a spectrum and range of possibilities and to feel at ease with this idea.

This awareness allows you to gauge, evaluate and calibrate in different situations and with different ideas, and people. As a result, you regain control, which is something students often reported as lacking during our conversations.

Developing a clear understanding of Mindfulness

When I trained in Mindfulness with MindSpace,[40] Adam Dacey taught me all that I am about to share with you. I learned how myself and many others lead very busy lives. When I train people in Mindfulness, be it students or staff, they often declare: 'I would practise Mindfulness if I had time but I am really busy', 'I have a lot to do.' We get up early in the morning, have a very quick breakfast. We rush out of the door to rush to work. During lunchtime, we eat a sandwich whilst checking emails or getting on with some work. When we come home in the evening when everything is done, we try to relax in front of a film or by surfing the net or by cracking open a bottle of wine (or all three at once).

Days, weeks, months and years go by like this, living on 'autopilot'. We know that we are alive but we are not aware of the present moment.

On autopilot, we don't realize that our mind is so busy. Buddhists call it the 'monkey mind' because it goes from one thought to the next like monkeys jump from one branch to the next. Restless! We fully associate with thoughts, feelings and emotions and don't even notice it!

What Mindfulness really means is being aware of our emotions, feelings, physical sensations and our environment, moment by moment. It gives us an opportunity to really experience life as it is. We become the observers of our lives. We take a step back and observe what is going on in our mind.

It also requires acceptance. This means that we need to pay attention to our thoughts and feeling without judging them as 'good' or 'bad'. Through Mindfulness we learn to tune in to what we are experiencing in the present moment rather than revisiting the past or imagining the future.

Mindfulness is in fact a series of meditations and we choose something in particular as the object of our focus and attention.

When we are training in Mindfulness, for example by learning to be mindful of sounds, we may notice that our mind becomes distracted by our thoughts, emotions and bodily sensations. This is completely normal when you first start. To remember that we are supposed to be focusing on sounds and returning our attention back to it is Mindfulness.

The practice of sitting and training in this way helps us to train in Mindfulness. It helps strengthen our ability to focus and through neuroplasticity, we can see how new parts of the brain develop. If we can practise regularly, ideally every day, we will be able to 'rewire' our brain and start seeing the benefits in our lives.

The four ingredients of Mindfulness

When you learn to become mindful, you will also notice that you:

• *Let go of your monkey mind and mental chatter*

As mentioned before, through Mindfulness it is easier to become increasingly able to observe thoughts and feelings. You will find it easier to notice and therefore distance yourself from constant mental chatter and thinking. You will become aware of the surprising amount of thoughts you have daily and how many come and go throughout the day. You will improve your ability to decide whether you want to engage with these thoughts, emotions, feelings and sensations, as opposed to being a victim and simply following them and engaging with them, making up stories and totally identifying with them.

• *Learn to live in the moment*

Lao Tzu (2009, p.49) said: 'if you are depressed, you are living in the past. If you are anxious, you are living in the future. If you are at peace, you are living in the present.'

If you stop and think about it, it makes sense. We have all experienced these anxious or depressed feelings whilst thinking about what happened to us, when we miss something or someone or when we anticipate or worry about something that might happen in the future. All you have that is guaranteed is this moment RIGHT NOW, reading this book or listening to the sounds around you, inside and outside the room you find yourself in; maybe you can hear a clock ticking? The now. This moment is the only thing guaranteed. The rest, the past, is gone forever and the future is yet to come... Why worry about it? Some people feel that it is not exciting enough to stay in the present and they enjoy the drama of discussing what might happen or what happened. But if you really stop and try, you will notice that the present holds a mysterious feeling, which is so strong and makes you feel so peaceful that any 'drama' will pale in comparison and seem worthless.

- *Give up judgement*

As Jon Kabat-Zinn (1994, p.8) states, paying attention non-judgementally means that we stop having strong opinions ('this is good', 'this is bad') about what happens in our lives; instead, we accept that things are the way they are. There is no point in fighting against what is because it will not change it. It is useful to learn to be alert and to stay with whatever is happening in the present moment. We often get angry, annoyed and frustrated very quickly, almost on autopilot. Mindfulness gives us the ability to respond to and accept things as they are. The reality is that we cannot change things most of the time. Because as Heraclitus said, 'Change is the only constant.' As human beings, we seem to spend so much time trying to change what we don't like or complaining about what is because we do not like it. All this energy spent like this is fruitless. It would be so much better to learn from nature and be more like animals and plants who simply are and enjoy the situation. In autumn, a leaf does not cling on to the branch because it does not want to fall. When it is ready to fall, it does so; the beauty is that this leaf will serve the tree because as it falls on the floor and starts decomposing, it will become compost for the same tree it was attached to not so long ago.

- *Develop detachment*

As you learn to practise non-judgement, you will also discover that it is easier to become detached from old views and perceptions. When you become the observer of your life and the present moment, you will discover that some ways of thinking are not useful anymore and you will be more able to let them go.

The benefits of having a regular Mindfulness practice

Over the last few years, many studies have empirically demonstrated and supported the advantages of Mindfulness. Whilst Siegel (2007b) highlights that activities such as yoga, t'ai chi and qigong are all practices and disciplines which encourage the cultivation of Mindfulness, the focus on this book will be on Mindfulness meditation. This is described by Walsh and Shapiro (2006, p.228) as a family of self-regulation practices that focus on training attention and awareness to bring mental processes under greater voluntary control and thereby foster general mental well-being and development and/or specific capacities such as calm, clarity and concentration. Shapiro and Carlson (2009) have suggested that Mindfulness meditation can also serve as a means of self-care to help combat burnout rates.

With more research, there is an increasing body of evidence-based affective, interpersonal and intrapersonal benefits of Mindfulness such as:

- *Emotion regulation*

Research carried out by Farb et al. (2007) and Williams (2010) suggests that Mindfulness meditation shifts individuals' ability to employ emotion regulation strategies that enable them to experience emotion selectively, and that the emotions they experience may be processed differently in the brain.

Emotion regulation has such strong empirical support as a benefit of Mindfulness meditation that recently the term 'mindful emotion regulation' was coined to refer to 'the capacity to remain mindfully aware at all times, irrespective of the apparent valence or magnitude of any emotion that is experienced' (Chambers et al. 2009, p.569).

- *Decreased emotional reactivity and increased response flexibility*

Findings in several studies carried out by Ortner et al. (2007) suggest that Mindfulness meditation practice may help individuals disengage from emotionally upsetting stimuli, enabling attention to be focused on the cognitive task at hand. They also support the notion that Mindfulness meditation decreases emotional reactivity.

Mindfulness enables us to become more mindful of our everyday activities: more present, in the moment. Most of our time is spent either in the future or the past, which leads to anxiety because of the gap between the NOW and where our mind is. We are missing a lot of our life. Mindfulness brings us to the present moment. It is important to remember that whilst it is important to spend some time observing our thoughts, emotions and feelings and to do some introspection, the purpose of life is to be lived and experienced. As human beings, our primary focus is to live our experiences and our lives fully, exchange with others, love and be loved.

It makes you notice your thoughts, feelings and emotions and makes you realize that YOU are SEPARATE from them. They are just that: a thought, a feeling or an emotion

You are one thought away from changing your life, if you so desire!

- *It helps relieve stress and anxiety as you become the observer of your life and untangle yourself from thoughts, feelings and emotions*

By training in Mindfulness meditation, it is possible to learn and develop the ability to detach from our thoughts, feelings and emotions and to be peaceful and calm instead. Participants in my courses report being able to notice the habits they have created around their thoughts and feelings and feel much more empowered to change them.

A recent meta-analysis of 39 studies supports the efficacy of Mindfulness-based therapy for reducing anxiety and depression symptoms (Hoffman et al. 2010). In addition, a study of Chinese college students by Tang et al. (2007) strengthens the above ideas by indicating that those students who were randomly assigned to participate in a Mindfulness meditation intervention had lower depression and anxiety, as well as less fatigue, anger and stress-related cortisol compared to a control group.

- *It allows you to become aware of people around you and develop greater empathy and compassion*

Part of the sitting practice helps us to become less focused on ourselves. We can forget our own worries and issues. As a result, we are naturally more focused on what other people are saying. We become better listeners as we are in the present moment. We can hear what people are saying instead of waiting to say our piece. This will definitely improve our relationships.

For example, Wang (2007) used a passive design and found that therapists who were experienced Mindfulness meditators scored higher on measures of self-reported empathy than therapists who did not meditate.

In addition to empathy, another characteristic that seems to derive from meditation is compassion. Kingsbury (2009) investigated the role of self-compassion in relation to Mindfulness. Two components of Mindfulness, non-judging and non-reacting, were strongly correlated with self-compassion, and two dimensions of empathy, taking on others' perspectives (i.e. perspective taking) and reacting to others' affective experiences with discomfort. Self-compassion fully mediated the relationship between perspective taking and Mindfulness.

Exercise 1 – Mindfulness and the meditation on sounds

This meditation focuses us on the sounds around us – in and outside the room we are in. We simply concentrate on what we hear – we become aware, notice and let go until another sound reaches our ears. We do not make up stories or engage with any of the sounds but use them as the central point of our attention. If a sensation, an emotion or a bodily sensation diverts our attention, we simply notice, acknowledge, let go and bring our attention back to the sounds. We do this over and over again. That's the practice.

Now have a go:

The ideal situation would be for you to find a comfortable place where you will not be disturbed and listen to the MP3.

To download the MP3 for this meditation – visit www. flourishingeducation.co.uk or email me.

If you do not have the MP3 simply follow these steps:

Ensure that you have your feet flat on the floor or if you are doing this lying down that your back is straight, shoulders gently relaxed. Gently close your eyes. If you don't feel comfortable closing your eyes, just focus your gaze about one metre away from you – a gentle gaze. Listen to the sounds around you. The focus – you are focused on what you can hear around you. We are not making up stories about these sounds. We simply notice, acknowledge and welcome them and then let them go and move to the following sound we can hear. If your mind has gone off on a tangent or you are being distracted by a thought, a sensation in your body or an emotion, simply become aware, notice, acknowledge the object of distraction and bring your attention back to the sounds. You do this over and over again. That's the practice. I would recommend starting with a three- or five-minute meditation. If you are doing this by yourself, you can use a timer.

Exercise 2 – Mindfulness and meditation on emotions – emotions as our friends

This meditation focuses on our emotions. We bring back a memory that generates emotions (they don't have to be too strong), which we would normally label as 'good' or 'bad'. We then imagine taking them out of our body and observing them. Do they have a colour, a shape? Do they move? Are they cold or hot? We befriend our emotions and notice where they sit in our body so that next time we experience a similar sensation, we will remember that it is our friend.

Once you have finished, write down how you are feeling. Are there any changes in the way you feel before and after? How do you find Mindful Listening AND Mindful Emotions? Reflect on what you learned today. Do you have a preference? Remember, it is YOUR practice and your strategies so be curious and look for what works best for you.

Now have a go:

Read the following instructions and then try this exercise for yourself:

Find a comfortable position with your feet flat on the floor. Gently close your eyes and take a nice deep breath. And again. For a minute or so focus on the sounds around you (same exercise as mindful awareness). Now, bring a memory of something that you would use to describe being 'happy': it can be an event that makes you really smile or a person. It can even be the best day of your life so far. Notice what you see, feel and hear as you recall the situation and identify where you feel this emotion in your body.

Once you have a strong connection with the emotion, imagine that you can take this emotion out of your body. Look at it. Does it have a shape? A colour? Movement? Is it hot or cold? This is your specific representation of 'happiness'. It is specific to you as a unique individual as others might not represent it in the same way as you do. Get acquainted with it and become friends with it.

You can then do the same thing with other emotions such as 'anger', 'sadness', 'pride', 'stress', and so on.

The beauty of this exercise is that it shows you that you don't have to be experiencing an event to feel the emotions. Memories trigger the same sensations. The more we befriend our emotions and get to know them, the more we become comfortable with them as and when they arise in our bodies.

Our emotions are simply a prediction based on our internal response or bodily sensation driven by past experiences of similar events and situations to the said event or situation. They are giving us a good indication of how we view the event and what our thinking is. Sometimes we may not notice the thoughts, but the emotions will be very obvious to us. Allowing all emotions – even those that we label as 'bad' – in our life is really important. As human beings we have a tendency to want to hang on to good emotions and to push back 'bad' ones, such as anger or sadness. But energy simply is energy in motion.

You can download the MP3 by visiting our website.

Exercise 3

Ask students to draw their own emotion(s) based on Exercise 2.

Exercise 4

Ask students: what would you say to your best friend about this situation?

Write down what you believe that people you love or your best friend would say to describe you and your qualities.

Exercise 5

Ask students: what can you control? What can't you? How can you enhance your control in these areas? It is empowering for students.

Physical health

Without our bodies, we would not be having a physical experience. It is therefore extremely important to learn to take care of ourselves and our bodies. In 2021, the UK Chief Medical Officers' Physical Activity Guidelines[41] were for adults to be active every day and to accumulate at least 150 minutes (2.5 hours) of moderate intensity activity (such as brisk walking or cycling); or 75 minutes of vigorous-intensity activity (such as running) per week.

Warburton et al. (2006) state that there is irrefutable evidence of the effectiveness of regular physical activity in the primary and secondary prevention of several chronic diseases (e.g. cardiovascular disease, diabetes, cancer, hypertension, obesity, depression and osteoporosis) and premature death.

These activities involve exercise and physical activity focusing on strength, flexibility and endurance. These could be leisurely activities such as walking or cycling or structured exercise (strength training, running or sport).

Physical health also includes nutrition and diet, involving our intake of nutrients and fluids and ensuring that we have a healthy digestion. Recommendations for a healthy diet suggest that it contains a balanced amount of nutrients such as carbohydrates, proteins, fats, vitamins and minerals.

Physically healthy individuals tend to avoid or reduce their consumption of alcohol and drugs as they report being conscious of the effect of these in their lives. They also practise self-care, which means looking after themselves when they have a cold or are unwell, ensuring that they rest and drink plenty of water, for example.

Many researchers suggest that having between seven and eight hours of undisturbed sleep is the answer to well-being. Rest and sleep did form an important part of the students' daily activities when I interviewed them. They demonstrated that they were conscious that having good sleep and rest hygiene helped them to remain physically healthy. For me, sleep is probably the recurring factor that highlighted the difference between flourishing and languishing students. Those who flourish tend to report sleeping soundly and feeling well and not tired ('*I feel refreshed after a good night's sleep*') upon waking up. To the contrary, languishing students reported not being able to sleep well or not being able to sleep at all, or even staying up all night because they were gaming. When we know and understand what happens to our brains through sleep, we clearly understand how vital and powerful sleep is.

Students could also clearly recognize that there is a difference between a resourceful and unresourceful state or behaviour; they seemed to be able to identify healthy and unhealthy coping strategies.

For example, one student declared that when she was at the height of her stress, she drank a whole bottle of wine every single night. Initially, she didn't see that it was an 'unresourceful behaviour' but with time and as we talked she became aware that 'behind every behaviour is a positive intent' and that she was using her drinking to relieve some of her stress and anxiety. She decided to change this habit by going to the gym, for a walk or by having a cup of tea instead. Of course, it was not easy to do but she has since reported being more able to consciously choose whether she has a drink or not. Not simply because it is something she always does when she gets back from university, after a stressful day, but because she really wants to. She also tries to enjoy the glass of wine much more.

Specific tools for the teacher:

Exercise 1 – Mindfulness and walking meditation – movement meditation

Walking meditation is an example of bringing Mindfulness into daily activities. It is a very simple technique that we can engage in every day and experience immediate results of what it means to be in the present moment.

The same principles can be applied to all the movements you make – when you move your arms or when you sit down. The essence is to bring Mindfulness into an act that normally we do quite mechanically and automatically. Very often when we are walking, we are completely focused on what we are going to say when we get to our destination and what we imagine the other person is going to say and what we will respond to them. Or we are completely focused on what happened in a previous situation, ruminating and rehashing old thoughts. Thus, we miss the experience of going from A to B: everything that is going on around us in the moment – the trees, the people around us.

In this exercise, we bring awareness into the body, focusing our attention on this current moment and this experience. Our focus is on the movements. We will do this practice with our eyes open. We can be in touch with all the sensations in our body and at the same time practise what we have learned and be aware of the sounds around us, the people around us, and so on.

We bring our energy down. We don't look at our feet. We just experience our feet from the sensations of our feet.

Now have a go:

Read the following instructions and then try this exercise for yourself:

Find a comfortable position with your feet flat on the floor. We will be doing this exercise standing up but as it is a movement meditation, it can be used with any movement you make. You can even use this when you brush your teeth. Simply focus on the movement of the toothbrush on each tooth and your hand gestures.

Gently close your eyes and take a nice deep breath. We will start this exercise by 'decomposing' our walking and noticing how many of the movements required to walk are automated in our lives. Of course, this is a good thing, as we wouldn't want to have to think about every single step we take, as it would use up too much of our energy. Now imagine you are about to take a step forward: notice how the weight of your body shifts to one leg, notice how your balance is affected and then put your foot forward and down and take a second step with the other leg. Play around with this exercise for a while, with your eyes open first and then with your eyes closed. Become aware of what is going on inside your body.

Once you have done this, you can start walking around – it can be indoors or outside. Simply focus on the following: lift, shift, forward, step; lift, shift, forward, step, etc.

Walk slowly and focus on feeling your feet from your feet rather than from the 'thought' of your feet.

If outside, you may get distracted by what you can hear (birds singing) or see or by your thoughts and emotions. In the same way you did with the other exercises, simply bring your attention back to each step. Not the one you have just taken or the next one but this one, in the present moment and in the now because that is the only guarantee we have in life.

You can download the MP3 by visiting our website.

If sleep is an issue for you, I would really recommend the work by Dr Huberman. You can check out his podcast called *Master your sleep*.[42] He provides a 10-minute and 35-minute Yoga Nidra script to use at the start or the end of the day. Very simple yet so powerful! I've started using it myself and I feel calmer as a result. These tools seem to provide benefits not just for sleep but also as a way to relax our sympathetic nervous system, which you will remember tends to trigger our 'fight-or-flight' response.

Exercise 2 – Mindful eating/drinking – how to appreciate our food and drinks

How often do you actually eat your sandwiches whilst working at your desk or drink your cup of tea/coffee whilst getting on with some work or watching TV?

We eat and drink every day so it is good to use these opportunities to gain an experience of the present moment. This exercise encourages us to let go of our mobiles and other distractions. We put them down and focus solely on one thing: what we are about to eat or to drink and nothing else.

Now you have a go:

Take a piece of chocolate – if it is wrapped take some time opening it. Think about how many people were involved to get this chocolate in your hand and send them all your thanks for making it possible. Now put the chocolate in your hand. Notice any urges or thoughts that come up. Do you feel like eating it quickly? Pick it up and smell it. What can you smell? Does it make your mouth water? Think about the ingredients – cocoa beans – where are they from? Who picked them? And so on, and again bring gratitude for the sun, the rain as well as all the resources and people required to make this piece of chocolate.

Finally, put the piece of chocolate in your mouth and simply let it melt slowly. Notice the flavours in your mouth and any 'mental chatter' going on. Bring your attention back to the sensations. When you have finished eating the piece of chocolate, open your eyes.

Notice how you are feeling? Do you want to eat another piece or another chocolate?

Very often when we eat or drink mindfully, we do not want to eat a whole bar of chocolate in five seconds. We start really appreciating what we put in our mouths.

This exercise can be done every time you drink or eat something.

In my workshop, I often also include a raisin for mindful eating and I go through exactly the same steps.

You can download the MP3 by visiting our website.

Exercise 3 – Simple health questionnaire – how to make students aware of their habits

This simple questionnaire has been used as part of the research for this book. It is heavily inspired and adapted from the research carried out by Jim Loehr and Tony Schwartz on the consulting they have done with the world's greatest athletes. In their book *The Power of Full Engagement* (2003), they explain that energy, not time, is the fundamental currency of high performance and that it is an even more precious resource that we need to manage well.

These questions encourage students to reflect on and become aware of their habits. It asks them to reflect on their physical activities, the amount of alcohol/drugs they consume every week, and so on. The aim is not to make them feel bad or guilty but to really encourage them to make changes in their daily routine to introduce more physical and healthier activities and habits.

Now you have a go:

On a scale of one to ten (one being never or very rarely and ten being all the time or almost all the time), indicate your level of agreement with the following statements:

Physical activities	
I have a high level of physical energy	Scale: 1 2 3 4 5 6 7 8 9 10
When I wake up, I feel rested and ready for a new day	Scale: 1 2 3 4 5 6 7 8 9 10
I like exercising and do so regularly every week	Scale: 1 2 3 4 5 6 7 8 9 10
My eating and drinking habits are healthy	Scale: 1 2 3 4 5 6 7 8 9 10
My routines for exercising are well set up	Scale: 1 2 3 4 5 6 7 8 9 10
I have regular 'rests' where I simply 'am'	Scale: 1 2 3 4 5 6 7 8 9 10
I sleep at least seven hours almost every day	Scale: 1 2 3 4 5 6 7 8 9 10
I feel fit and healthy	Scale: 1 2 3 4 5 6 7 8 9 10
I know what to do to recharge my batteries	Scale: 1 2 3 4 5 6 7 8 9 10
Mental activities	
I find it easy to concentrate and focus on my work	Scale: 1 2 3 4 5 6 7 8 9 10
I manage my time effectively and well	Scale: 1 2 3 4 5 6 7 8 9 10
I have a positive outlook on life	Scale: 1 2 3 4 5 6 7 8 9 10
I try to find solutions to problems and issues	Scale: 1 2 3 4 5 6 7 8 9 10

I can easily switch off when not studying/working	Scale: 1 2 3 4 5 6 7 8 9 10
I like to think about things	Scale: 1 2 3 4 5 6 7 8 9 10
Emotional activities	
I can recognize and name my positive and negative emotions	Scale: 1 2 3 4 5 6 7 8 9 10
I am happy with all my emotions (negative and positive) and welcome them	Scale: 1 2 3 4 5 6 7 8 9 10
I can regulate my emotions and can express them in a healthy way	Scale: 1 2 3 4 5 6 7 8 9 10
I feel connected to others and know who to reach out to when I am feeling sad or upset	Scale: 1 2 3 4 5 6 7 8 9 10
Social activities	
I create good relationships with others	Scale: 1 2 3 4 5 6 7 8 9 10
I get along with my friends	Scale: 1 2 3 4 5 6 7 8 9 10
I get along with my family	Scale: 1 2 3 4 5 6 7 8 9 10
I feel confident	Scale: 1 2 3 4 5 6 7 8 9 10
I feel that I can share with others easily	Scale: 1 2 3 4 5 6 7 8 9 10
I can manage conflict and focus on a positive outcome for all involved	Scale: 1 2 3 4 5 6 7 8 9 10

Spiritual activities	
I have a passion/hobby I engage with on a regular basis	Scale: 1 2 3 4 5 6 7 8 9 10
I know what I want to achieve in life	Scale: 1 2 3 4 5 6 7 8 9 10
I have a sense of purpose in life and/or I know why I chose the course I did.	Scale: 1 2 3 4 5 6 7 8 9 10
I know what my personal values are in life	Scale: 1 2 3 4 5 6 7 8 9 10
I set goals which are aligned with these personal values	Scale: 1 2 3 4 5 6 7 8 9 10
I have a fulfilling life	Scale: 1 2 3 4 5 6 7 8 9 10
I enjoy reconnecting to nature on a regular basis	Scale: 1 2 3 4 5 6 7 8 9 10
I believe I am learning and growing every day	Scale: 1 2 3 4 5 6 7 8 9 10
I believe I am a compassionate human being	Scale: 1 2 3 4 5 6 7 8 9 10

Exercise 4 – Identification of resourceful and unresourceful coping strategies

Once they have filled in the questionnaire, students are encouraged to identify their healthy and unhealthy coping strategies. What do they do when they are feeling stressed? Go out and drink alcohol, use drugs, stay in and don't talk to others? It will enable them to be honest and open and to really look at their behaviours in a different light. Remind them that these behaviours are not bad nor good; they are just coping strategies which I would simply call unresourceful. It is possible to find another strategy which is much more resourceful.

Social health

In the *Sane Society*, Fromm (2001, p.13) explains that all human beings have 'the need for relatedness, transcendence, rootedness, the need for a sense of identity and the need for a frame or orientation and devotion'.

Students that I would describe as flourishing surround themselves with supportive people and possess the ability to develop satisfying interpersonal relationships with others. During our conversations, they also reported a greater ability to adapt comfortably to various social settings and act appropriately in a variety of situations.

On the other hand, students who would be considered as 'languishing' reported feeling lonely and not feeling part of a community; they felt unable to create meaningful relationships. They often feel isolated and cannot see or recognize how they are contributing or making an impact on the community. They also report feeling different and invisible to others. This is particularly heightened when they come from a different educational background or class.

It is extremely important for students and HE institutions to be conscious of this aspect. When first-year students transition from secondary school to university, they arrive in a completely new environment and are put in halls of residence or in accommodation with people they don't know. If students are unable to form satisfying interpersonal relationships with others where they live and on their course, this will have a very detrimental effect on their university experience and student life. This sets up a bad and negative experience with the 'university'. Some languishing students said that at times they feel that *'no one here cares about me'*.

There is a clear need for institutions and students to ensure that they are integrated into the university community. When I talked with students, they discussed the impact of exclusion (whether real or imagined) on their well-being and on their university achievements. For example, two or three students I interviewed insisted on bringing up the issues they experienced when they first arrived at university and were told that there was no space in halls for them; they were put in accommodation with postgraduate students with whom they had nothing in common. Students highlighted the importance of having a sense of belonging at university. They told me that initially they didn't have this sense of belonging because they were so frightened and felt that they didn't fit in. They were worried that no one was going to understand how they were feeling and how much they dreaded the loneliness. Peplau and Perlman (1982) defined loneliness as the aversive state experienced when a discrepancy exists between the interpersonal relationships one wishes to have and those that one perceives one currently has.

Students I talked to also expressed that when they are feeling stressed or reporting feeling stressed, it becomes a threat to healthy relationships and prevents them from going out and socializing, thus turning the situation into a vicious circle. They reported a focus on themselves rather than on others. Some students also mentioned that when they are having a difficult time, they do not really want to talk to others about their situation or their experience; they simply want to sleep or be on their own. Therefore, there's a real focus on the self versus a focus on others.

Fromm-Reichmann (1959, p.3) sheds light on these feelings and helps us understand where they stem from when he states that:

> the longing for interpersonal intimacy stays with every human being from infancy throughout life; and there is no human being who is not threatened by its loss... the human being is born with the need for contact and tenderness.

Strong social skills and good communication skills are required by students to flourish. Training and tips on how to develop such skills would be beneficial to students. Mindfulness may also help us as academic tutors to develop empathy towards our students and in turn for students to develop self-empathy and empathy for others.

In 2006, Aiken carried out a qualitative study of therapists who were experienced meditators and found that they believed that Mindfulness meditation helped develop empathy towards clients. Interviews were conducted with six psychotherapists who each had more than ten years of experience practising both therapy and Mindfulness meditation. Consistent themes from the data indicated that Mindfulness helps therapists develop their ability to experience and communicate a felt sense of clients' inner experiences; be more present to clients' suffering and help clients express their bodily sensations and feelings.

This same practice may also enable students to learn to be more accepting of the situation, of others and how they behave without wanting to change who they are. It may also enable them to take responsibility for their feelings and gain a sense of accountability.

Research suggests that cooperation may motivate prosocial behaviour by influencing psychological states that support generosity and cooperation. For example, Dunn and Schweitzer (2005, Study 3) found that participants who described a time in the past when they felt grateful towards someone (thereby creating grateful emotion in the present) subsequently reported higher levels of trust towards a third party than did participants who were asked to describe a time they felt angry, guilty or proud.

Emmons and McCullough (2003) also found that participants who wrote on a daily basis for two weeks about things for which they were grateful reported offering more emotional support and (with near-statistical significance) tangible help to others than did participants who wrote about their daily hassles or about ways in which they were more fortunate than others.

If the effects of gratitude on psychological well-being (Emmons and McCullough 2003) are due to real (or even merely perceived) changes in people's social relationships, and if positive social relations are conducive to health and well-being, then Mindfulness and the gratitude meditation might be a good activity for students and members of staff alike.

Specific tools for the teacher:

Exercise 1 – Mindfulness and gratitude meditation – developing gratitude for everything/everyone in your life

Cicero stated that 'Gratitude is not only the greatest of the virtues but the parent of all others' (2004, p. 37).

If we reflect on what we don't have, this leads to unhappiness. This meditation will do the opposite and will encourage us to focus on all the positive aspects in our life. Our experience of happiness in the world depends upon the response that we give to our life and our life events, not what is actually happening in our life. It is all down to our state of mind and mental habits.

Nothing less, nothing more. We can increase our experience of happiness not necessarily by manipulating our external environment but simply by changing our mind and, most importantly, by focusing on all the good things we possess or experience.

Now you have a go:

Find a comfortable position with your feet flat on the floor. Gently close your eyes and take a nice deep breath. And again. For a minute or so focus on the sounds around you (same exercise as mindful awareness). Now, bring your attention inwards and focus on your breath, wherever you feel it the most in your body. For a minute focus on the sensation of the natural flow of your breath coming in and out of your body. Now, we will start with the gratitude practice. Focus on your body and think about all the parts of your body you are grateful for (your hands, legs, sense of touch, smell, hearing, particularly if you are lucky enough to be able to use these unaided).

You then start focusing on all the people in your life you are grateful for – loved ones, close relatives and family, friends and colleagues, acquaintances, people you meet in the street and even people who represent a challenge for you. Notice what sensations gratitude generates in your body. When we feel genuinely grateful for things/people in our lives, it creates a lovely sensation in our bodies.

You can download the MP3 by visiting our website.

Exercise 2 – The gratitude daily challenge

As mentioned before, gratitude helps us feel happier and appreciating what we have in our life really helps. This gratitude daily challenge involves a quick exercise every morning and afternoon. Simply spend several mornings when you first wake up and last thing at night to find three to five new things to be grateful for every day. It helps to also do it at the end of the day and to review what went well in your day, what you would do differently and to focus on specific events and people. You can also start every day when you wake up by saying to yourself: 'Yes, another day on planet earth!' I introduced this exercise to my life at the beginning of the first lockdown and it has been a game changer. I also then move my toes and fingers and reflect on how I will be able to get out of bed unaided (which is more than so many people in the world). When we truly connect and experience gratitude, we experience a really positive emotional response. You can achieve this by focusing on the sensation that this gratitude produces in your body.

Spiritual health

Egan et al. (2011) declared that 'spirituality means different things to different people. It may include (a search for) one's ultimate beliefs and values, a sense of meaning and purpose in life, a sense of connectedness, identity and awareness and for some people religion' (p.309).

Banks (1998) referred to the principle of Universal Mind to explain 'spiritual health', describing it as the formless energy that animates all of life – the intelligent life energy behind human psychological functioning.

For me, spiritual health is linked to the sense we give to things and life. There is something more than just getting up in the morning, going to work, eating and then going to bed. There is a deeper sense to our existence. Maybe it could be described as a sense of belonging to something bigger? Our society has standards and ideas of success, which suggest that to be happy we need to get the degree, get the job, get the car, then get a better job with more money, get a house, get married, etc. There is a sense of emptiness when we realize that a good job, good money, a big house and car with lots of holidays does not mean that we will be happy. It gives some of us a sense of emptiness because we lack a sense of purpose and a life mission. Some students said that they often asked themselves – why am I here? What do I love and what impact do I want to make with my life?

Macmin and Foskett (2004) highlight the fact that spirituality is an issue that individuals and communities are asking to be recognized in various contexts and in particular mental health.

Spiritual health is a personal matter involving values and beliefs that provide purpose to our lives. Whilst different individuals may have different views of what spiritual health is, it is generally considered to be the search for meaning and purpose in human existence. It leads us to strive for a state of harmony with ourselves and others, and a balance between our inner needs and the rest of the world.

This spiritual health can be linked to religion or to the idea that there is something bigger than us. It can also simply be a need to be connected to nature and be outside (in a field, a forest, etc.) but most importantly it is that sense of knowing that there are things we would like to achieve in life. An area of interest or topics for which we have developed a real passion and that we can imagine ourselves spending a lot of time doing (even if we are not paid for it).

Spiritual health also leads to compassion as it makes us appreciate what we have in our lives and the advantages we have in comparison to others.

In my humble opinion, spiritual health is the most over-looked and least discussed 'health'. So many of the flourishing students I interviewed told me about their sense of 'purpose' or 'finding meaning' in what they are doing. This is true for students studying to become engineers or doctors. When a student knows what they want to do as a job, they tap into the intrinsic motivation we discussed before. But spiritual health has also been reported by others as '*a feeling that I belong to something bigger. I get this sense when I go in the park and watch squirrels going up and down the trees or when I go for a walk in nature.*' The final way to report spiritual health is '*a belief in God*'.

The 13 new interviews I carried out with students showed me that the higher the spiritual health, the less the individualism. One student told me that they wanted to become a doctor and that it'd been something they'd wanted to do since they were very little because '*it's a good cause where I can bring benefit to a larger group, to a whole community*'. Another student said that '*I want to work for an NGO and use my language skills for the greater good.*'

It seems to me that these students' aims are not simply to achieve their goals or to gain their degree for their own benefit; it's not just about themselves. I have to admit that their thinking has deeply influenced me and since our conversations I too have decided to move away from the 'what's important to me' and the more 'me-centred' approach I had in life to a move to bring change into education. This book is a modest stride in this direction and it feels really good. I would really encourage you to try it. I promise: it won't disappoint!

A little caveat regarding 'life purpose' and 'destination'. In the last few months, I have spoken to many young people who get really upset and even annoyed by the notion that they should absolutely know what they want to 'do' or 'be' later on in life. The notion of 'destination' with the idea that one should aim for the holy grail that is university (preferably Cambridge and Oxford) and therefore consider this when choosing their GCSE or A-level options is having a very negative impact on their well-being. One student told me: *'I don't feel I have a choice. This is the path I am told I have to follow.'* This is clearly miles away from what I have described above. So let's be crystal clear. Spiritual health is not about knowing for sure what we want to do when we grow up. I don't think I know what I want to be when I grow up! Spiritual health is getting to know what feels good and right for us in a given moment, as well as perhaps knowing what we might want to do as a profession. We know it's spiritual health because the exploration is enjoyable. It's about the journey not the destination. As one of the interviewees put it: *'it's about the process. I am enjoying the different classes and the different topics I am currently studying because I want to figure out if I would like to be a heart specialist, an anaesthetist, or a GP. I'm not sure yet.'*

Specific tools for the teacher:

Exercise 1 – Life purpose exercise

This exercise involves sitting down and thinking about the type of life you truly want. It can be done once a year or more regularly – every three or six months. It can be done on your own or by enlisting the help of someone else and consists of identifying several time frames (short/medium/long term) and all the areas of your life you would like to explore (e.g. professional/financial/family, etc.).

Now you have a go:

Areas of your life	Short term	Medium term	Long term
University	Write plan for essay	Write 2,000-word essay for end of term	Pass my first year with 2:1 overall grades

Once the exercise is done, you can simply let go of the outcome and ask yourself what the first step to get you there is. Start with that task and then with the next one, and so on. It's not about getting there; it's about enjoying it along the way. You can download the PDF by visiting our website.

Exercise 2 – Mindfulness and meditation on Loving Kindness – bringing compassion to oneself and others

The Dalai Lama said that 'love and compassion are necessities, not luxuries. Without them humanity cannot survive' (1999, p.59) This meditation is also called Metta. This is the Sanskrit word for the practice of Loving Kindness. We simply develop the wish for everyone to be happy, including ourselves. This is also called compassion and to apply true compassion we need to commit and apply it to everyone and everything around us. Our compassionate attitude does not change when we believe someone is behaving in a negative way. It is a mental attitude based on the wish for others to be free from their suffering and to be able to overcome their problems. It is also linked to a sense of commitment, responsibility and respect towards others.

We develop a state of mind that can include a wish for good things for oneself. In developing Loving Kindness or compassion, we begin with the wish to be free of suffering and then take that natural feeling towards oneself and cultivate it, enhance it and extend it to include and encompass others.

Now have a go:

Read the following instructions and then try this exercise for yourself:

Find a comfortable position with your feet flat on the floor. Gently close your eyes and take a nice deep breath. And again. For a minute or so focus on the sounds around you (same exercise as mindful awareness). Now, bring your attention inwards and focus on your breath, wherever you feel it the most in your body. For a minute focus on the sensation of the natural flow of your breath coming in and out of your body. You will start with a specific mantra. Start with yourself because if you are suffering, you cannot help anybody else and say: 'may I be secure, be happy, be healthy, live well'. Repeat this for a minute or so and then bring up someone whom you love or respect greatly and say: 'may you be secure, be happy, be healthy, live well'. Then extend this to a work colleague or someone you know but not as well; then do the same with someone you find challenging and with whom you don't really get on with. If you are unable to send them good wishes, then at this point, you are the one suffering and the one in need of loving kindness and compassion and so say again: 'may I be secure, be happy, be healthy, live well'. The person you don't get on with is not here with you and they are probably unaware that you have these feelings or emotions towards them so what is the point of keeping them inside yourself as you are just punishing yourself instead? Nelson Mandela said it beautifully: 'Resentment is like drinking/taking poison and then hoping it will kill your enemies.'

Finish this exercise by sending loving kindness to everybody around you – in front of you, behind you, to the sides (left and right), above and below us (this also includes animals) by saying: 'may you all be secure, be happy, be healthy, live well'.

You can download the MP3 by visiting our website.

As mentioned previously, flourishing students mention five different competencies that I would now like to explore in turn. When I first wrote the book, I didn't realize that these were in fact five of the nine competencies that culturally agile individuals possess, as presented by Professor Paula Caliguiri in her latest book *Build Your Cultural Agility*.[43] Cultural agility follows the concept of physical agility and is described by Caliguiri as 'the ability to be comfortable and effective in situations of cultural novelty. As a mix of "nature and nurture", our personality, knowledge, motivation and experiences all combine in a unique way to create our current level of cultural agility' (2021, p.15). This is really exciting and great news because we can indeed change our level of cultural agility. As academics and parents, we can tap into Caliguiri's work and empower young people to understand why they might be experiencing culture shock when they arrive in a new environment and most importantly, we can teach them how to develop or build these competencies. This is what I did during lockdown with a group of Sixth Form students and their response has been extremely positive. One student told me that *it was a real eye-opening experience*. Another participant added: 'I have learnt lots of different ways to handle change and to relax more. I have also discovered a lot about myself.'

So what are these five specific competencies? Let's take a look at each one in turn.

Openness

Openness refers both to experiences and people. It means that we are interested in discovering and experiencing new and different things than in the past. We also tend to be interested in others and to be more open to who they are, what they do and their beliefs or values. Going back to the metaphor of the flower, it suggests that as a flower we accept the other flowers standing next to us or in the garden.

Recent studies have indicated that factors other than intelligence, such as two out of the Big Five personality traits (conscientiousness and openness), are useful predictors of academic performance (Chamorro-Premuzic and Furnham 2003a, 2003b).

McCrae and Costa's (1987) Five Factor Model measures broad factors such as openness to experience and reported that the following adjectives best characterize openness: 'original, imaginative, broad interests and daring' (p.87).

Students who participated in my eight-week Mindfulness workshops reported being more open to others and to diverse experiences. For example, one student in particular stated that they were more engaged with the challenges they faced, knowing that these would not be there forever. They were more able to receive information about themselves (e.g. getting feedback) and thus reported that they felt less defensive. Most importantly, they were able to maintain greater emotional balance when faced with stressful and difficult situations. They could notice their negative thoughts and emotions and were able to distance themselves from them rather than automatically engaging and identifying with them.

Curiosity

What is curiosity?

Curiosity is defined by the Oxford Dictionary as 'a strong desire to learn or know something'.

Caliguiri notes that it is 'a motivation or desire to seek and find answers and works in our lives very much like a flashlight would in a dark room. Without it we would trip over a lot of obstacles in the room' (2021, p.45).

Being curious was expressed by the students I interviewed and colleagues as a real desire to know and understand. It seems to come naturally to them. It is a way of thinking that motivates us to go deeper, to analyse topics and concepts and to show interest. It was also described by a colleague as a way of questioning what is established by going beyond appearances and fixed concepts. Being curious is part of this thirst to learn, this thirst to discover, to be faced with something new, to question facts and to look for new information, observe and analyse.

The attributes of curious young people

The students who described themselves as curious also stated that they felt enthusiasm, a real desire to learn and discover new things, interest and even passion for the topic they studied at university. We can be curious about our culture, our beliefs, our differences and similarities, how things function and how useful they are or not. We can also question how certain aspects have a specific place in our lives and how we create them.

During the interviews carried out for this book, it would appear that curious students have a clear motivation to discover more about their topic and chosen field of study. They want to discover interesting facts and concepts and are not afraid to ask questions.

A note on some comments made by young people about their schooling and its impact on their level of curiosity. Several students I interviewed told me how they felt that when they were at secondary school, their 'curiosity wasn't truly encouraged'. 'I was told "great questions, but not now. There's no time for this right now."' Obviously, this is not a criticism of my colleagues. I understand how challenging it is when you have so much in the curriculum to 'cram in' to ensure the students are prepared for the exam. That said, given the importance of curiosity for our well-being and flourishing, it would be very good to foster curiosity more rather than 'killing it', which is what another interviewee said. They added: 'my curiosity slowly *died over the years. I wasn't interested in a lot of what I had to learn so I stopped asking questions because that wasn't what was rewarded in school.'*

Flexibility

What is flexibility?

The term flexibility is defined by the Oxford Dictionary as: 'The quality of bending easily without breaking. The ability to be easily modified. The willingness to change or compromise.'

Flexibility and adaptability seem to be two major competences that flourishing students possess. When I interviewed some students who were performing very well academically, they indicated that they learned very early on in their university life that these were two of the most important qualities a student must have. They also stated that they were both willing to change with or without notice, and that they had developed the ability to adapt to change (in their environment, their daily schedule and routine). The willingness to modify the way they worked through feedback was also something that flourishing students mentioned. They said it was difficult to receive feedback from tutors, and at times even intimidating, but that when they moved past the notion that it was a daunting task, they quickly realized that to perform better they had to receive feedback and integrate it into their next piece of work.

Most importantly, flexibility also requires a willingness to recognize the need for help and to accept it. Flexible students are happy to look for different solutions to their problems.

For me, this flexibility matches Caligiuiri's concept of tolerance of ambiguity or 'how comfortable we are in unpredictable, uncertain or ambiguous situations' (p.26). This tolerance of ambiguity has been linked by researcher Michael Frone with a greater ability to cope with the stress caused by working in a context with greater uncertainty.[44]

Resilience

What is resilience?

The term resilience stems from Latin (*resiliens*) and was originally used to refer to the pliant or elastic quality of a substance (Joseph 1994).

The Oxford Dictionary defines resilience as 'The capacity to recover quickly from difficulties; toughness' or 'the ability of a substance or object to spring back into shape; elasticity.'

I am not particularly keen on this definition because from my own experience, the changes didn't happen 'quickly' but over time. The same seems to be true for the students who shared their stories of resilience. There is also an issue with the idea of 'springing back into shape', as it would mean that the person reverts to their own 'state of being' without experiencing any personal and developmental changes.

My favourite definition is that of the American Psychological Association, which describes resilience as 'the process of adapting well in the face of adversity, trauma, tragedy, threats or significant sources of stress — such as family and relationship problems, serious health problems or workplace and financial stressors. It means "bouncing back" from difficult experiences.'[45]

The attributes of resilient young people

Benard (1991) argues that we are all born with innate resiliency, with the capacity to develop the traits commonly found in resilient survivors.

- *Social competence* (responsiveness, cultural flexibility, empathy, caring, communication skills and a sense of humour). She describes social competence as the ability to elicit positive responses from others, thus establishing positive relationships with both adults and peers.
- *Problem solving* (planning, help-seeking, critical and creative thinking); or the planning that facilitates seeing oneself in control and resourcefulness in seeking help from others.
- *Autonomy* (sense of identity, self-efficacy, self-awareness, task-mastery and adaptive distancing from negative messages and conditions); or a sense of one's own identity and an ability to act independently and exert some control over one's environment.
- *A sense of purpose and belief in a bright future* (goals, educational aspirations, persistence, hopefulness and a sense of a bright future).

Resilience is not a genetic trait that only a few of us possess but is our inborn capacity for self-righting (Werner and Smith 1992), transformation and change (Lifton 1993). Werner and Smith also declared that a resilient child is one 'who loves well, works well, plays well, and expects well' (p.192).

Resilience is really what helps us have a better-than-expected outcome after a difficult event. It generates protective factors or processes when facing difficulty and so is much more something we do than something we have.

In the book *Second Wave Positive Psychology*, Ivtzan et al. (2015) talk about three meanings of resilience:

1. Resistance resilience is being strong in the face of adversity.

2. Recovering resilience is being able to recover from adversity.

3. Reconfiguration resilience is where we are transformed by adversity in ways that bring benefits. This is also known as post-traumatic growth.

Differences between resilient and non-resilient people

There is neurological evidence to support the psychological data that show some people may be relatively high or low in resilience (Waugh et al. 2008).

Waugh et al. found that when people with higher resilience were shown a cue signalling there was an equal chance they would see a distressing picture or a neutral picture, they only exhibited neural reactions indicating an unpleasant emotional response if they actually saw the distressing picture. Resilient people also returned to baseline cardiac and neurological states sooner than those with low resilience when exposed to stressful situations (Waugh et al. 2008).

In contrast, participants with low resilience reacted to threats or even a possibility of threats sooner and for longer periods of time, as indicated by activity in the amygdala and insular areas of the brain (Waugh et al. 2008).

As academic tutors and members of staff, we can help our students change this. Neuroplasticity can be our ally. We can explain to students that neuroplasticity enables the brain to create new neural pathways by creating new connections between our neurons. Our brain then uses these pathways to act. They are installed through learning, education and by developing new habits. This means that it is possible for students to become more resilient.

Language

The language we use daily contributes to the way we interact with others and the world around us. Our words and expressions influence both our attitude and behaviours towards a situation or a person. The ability to speak is a power. With our words, we can do a lot of damage or we can soothe. We need to be aware and to discover the vocabulary we use and what impact it has on our body, mind and on others.

Useful presuppositions

When I trained as an NLP practitioner and Master practitioner, I was introduced to the NLP presuppositions. They form the central principles of NLP and come across in our lives through the language we use and our choices of words. They can be considered as the guiding philosophy or 'beliefs'. NLP does not claim that they are true or universal but they see them as a very useful 'working principle' to have in our life. Because we presuppose they are true, we act as if they were and start introducing them in our life. When I interviewed students and experts, although they did not 'voice' or 'express' these concepts in exactly this way, some of these presuppositions are helpful for students and can help them flourish.

Here are some of them.

- *People respond to their experience, not to reality itself. The map is not the territory.*

We do not know what reality is. Our senses, beliefs and past experience give us a map of the world from which to operate.

But a map is never completely accurate, otherwise it would be the same as the ground it covers. So, for example, a map of London is not the city of London itself. It is just a representation of its streets. Some maps are better than others for finding our way round. We will look at this in more detail when we talk about communication models and how we filter the information we receive.

- *Having a choice is better than not having a choice.*

Try to have a map of the world that gives you the widest number of choices. If you have no choice, you are dead. If you have two choices, you have a dilemma; if you have three choices or more, you have options. You will be freer as a result and have the ability to influence your life more.

- *People make the best choice they can at all times.*

We do the best we can with the resources we have in the moment. These choices may appear bizarre, unhelpful or evil to others but that might be the only way we can cope with a situation at a given point based on our 'maps of the world'. If we are given more choices or options, we can take them and change our behaviours and ways of thinking. I believe this is a particularly useful concept, as it reduces feelings of guilt and self-blame.

- *People work perfectly.*

Nobody is broken or wrong. Nobody needs mending. We are all executing our strategies effectively. Some of our strategies may be flawed or ineffective but they can be changed to something more useful and desirable.

- *All actions have a purpose.*

Our actions are not random. We are trying to achieve something, although we may not be aware of what it is.

- *Every behaviour has a positive intention.*

All our actions have at least one purpose – to make us happy. We tend to do things that we value and that benefit us. NLP separates the intention behind the action and the action itself. A person is not their behaviour. When a person has a better choice of behaviour that also achieves their positive intention, they will take it.

- *The unconscious mind balances the conscious; it is not malicious.*

The unconscious is everything that is not in consciousness at the present moment. It contains all the resources we need to live in balance.

- *The meaning of the communication is not simply what you intend, but also the response you get.*

The response you get from communication may be different from the one you wanted, but there are no failures in communication, only responses and feedback. If you are not getting the results you want, change what you are doing. Take responsibility for the way you communicate and for the result it creates.

- *We already have all the resources we need or we can create them.*

There are no unresourceful people, only unresourceful states of mind and they can be changed if we are aware of them.

- *Mind and body form a system. They are different expressions of one person.*

Mind and body interact and influence each other. It is not possible to make a change in one without the other being affected. When we think differently, our bodies change. When we act differently, we change our thoughts and our emotions (see neuroplasticity).

- *We process all information through our senses.*

Developing your senses so that they become more accurate gives you better information and helps you think more clearly.

- *Modelling successful performance leads to excellence.*

NLP is the study of excellence and was created by two Americans, John Grinder and Richard Bandler, who modelled three therapists – Virginia Satir (family therapist), Fritz Perls (father of Gestalt Therapy) and Milton Erickson (hypnotherapy). They believed that if one person can do something, then it is possible for another to model it and to teach it to others. In this way, everyone can learn to get better results in their own way. This is a bit what we are doing in this book. You do not become a clone of the person you are modelling; you discover their 'strategies' to deal with a situation or event and you adopt them in your life. You learn from them.

- *If you want to understand, act.*

The learning is in the doing.

- *There are no errors only learning. No mistakes only feedback.*

We do not make mistakes or errors which have a negative connotation. We learn and use the feedback to 'bridge the gap' between where we are and where we want to be.

- *If you always do what you've always done, then you will always get what you've always got.*

Pretty self-explanatory – if you carry on doing the same thing all the time, you will get the same results all the time.

- *It's not what happens to you that matters to you but what you do with it.*

As mentioned previously, we can choose our response to events – that's our response ability.

How we communicate

The NLP Communication model was developed by Tad James and Wyatt Woodsmall in 1988 based on the work initially produced by Grinder and Bandler in the 1970s. It uses many concepts of Cognitive Psychology and the work of linguists and analysts Alfred Korzybski (1933) and Noam Chomsky (1964).

We are constantly taking in information through our five senses and processing it. A lot of the information we receive takes place unconsciously. Consciously trying to process all the data received would not be possible and would require us to use too much energy. Therefore, our nervous system filters it.

The filters we use are based on the language we use, the words we use, our beliefs, memories, our unique experience (what happened to us in the past) and our metaprograms. Everyone filters and experiences any given situation differently. It's our internal representations (subjective perceptions) that determine how we view the world and everything we experience.

We then delete, distort or generalize information per our unique filters. Once incoming information passes through our filters, a thought is constructed. These thoughts create internal representations (or maps of the world). For example – read this and then close your eyes and try it out:

Think of a lemon – imagine that you have it in your hands and feel how heavy or light it is. Then take it up to your nose and smell it. Can you smell it? Now take a knife and hear the noise it makes as you cut it in half – notice the strong smell coming out of it. How do you feel? Now take one half and put it in your mouth. Taste the bitterness in your mouth. Remember last time you had a lemon like this.

This example demonstrates that we form internal representations which are effectively sensory perceptions such as a picture with sounds, emotions, smells and tastes. Our internal representations immediately trigger corresponding emotions, or 'states' as we call them in NLP jargon, which then impact on all our behaviours and on our physiology.

So, the reality that we experience is largely determined by what we do inside our heads.

Our language – a way of expressing our map of the world.

Observing your language or that of your students/colleagues might give you an indication of their preferences. Here are some examples:

Visual

I get the picture... I see what you mean... let's get this in perspective... it appears that... show me... the focus of attention... take a closer look... looking closer... it's clear to me... a different angle... this is the outlook... with hindsight... you'll look back on this.

Auditory

That rings a bell... we're on the same wavelength... let's talk about it... within earshot... let's discuss things... I'm speechless... shout from the hilltops... people will hear you... this silence is deafening... it's music to my ears... word for word... in a manner of speaking.

Kinaesthetic

He's thick skinned... a cool customer... I grasp your meaning... a heated argument... I will be in touch... I can't put my finger on it... we are scratching the surface... let's dig deeper... hit the nail on the head... I feel it in my stomach.

Olfactory/digital

It's a matter of taste... let's chew it over... I smell a rat... it's a bitter pill to swallow... that's an acid comment... it's a bit fishy... it leaves a bad taste.

Being aware of your own sensory preference and that of others can help us communicate better. If someone uses a lot of 'kinaesthetic' language, they are likely to respond better if you use the same language than if you use 'visual' words.

Language difference between the flourishing and the languishing student

During the interviews I carried out with the ten students, I noticed a major difference between the language used by students who were reporting feeling stressed and anxious or those who were not reporting major stress in their life.

- *I can't versus I can and it's possible as well as 'should versus could'*

When I replayed some of the interviews, I became aware that some students tended to have a much more negative view of the situation and they used modals such as 'I can't' and 'it's not possible'. In contrast, students who reported feeling more settled and having overcome some of their difficult experiences and situations used words such 'I can' and 'it's possible', 'I am going to try'. Those who said 'I can't' often added '*do it for me*' (with or without a please).

Others tended to use phrases such as 'I should be doing better', 'I should get on with my assignment or work', whereas others clearly focused on goals and what might be possible when considering future tasks: 'I could start working early'.

The use of words such as 'I can' seems to match the 'conscious autosuggestion' technique described by Coué in his books *Self Mastery Through Conscious Autosuggestion* (1922) and *How to Practice Suggestion and Autosuggestion* (1923), in which he stated that 'believing that the thing which you wish to do is easy, it becomes so for you, although it may appear difficult to others' (1923, pp.77–78).

• *Self-focused versus other-focused*

There is also a clear difference between the language focus of some students who tend to use I, me, myself, mine, and therefore are much more self-focused, and others who are much less self-focused and who discuss how their experience impacted on others and how others helped them.

It would be very interesting to explore this aspect further and to see whether these different uses of language impact on a student's ability to flourish in their environment.

PART III
THE TUTOR'S OWN TOOLBOX

Chapter 5

It all starts with you – the flourishing tutor

'Change starts with you'
– Einstein

In many HE institutions, the vision is to nurture skilled, adaptable and resilient graduates who can thrive in the global economy which is changing faster than ever. This means taking care of the student's well-being so that we can have a 'flourishing student'.

This concept is admirable and makes complete sense but it is also vital for staff to be 'flourishing' in their working environment and to focus on their well-being. There is therefore a real need for a 'positive staff experience' too. If we go back to the Flourishing Model (FM), it does not simply apply to students but also to us. We are part of a system and as such our own stress level will affect others around us. Very often, as teachers and tutors, we tend to forget our own health and don't take care of ourselves as well as we recommend others to do for themselves.

Of course, when I talk with colleagues, it is obvious to me that we understand that taking time to relax, eat well, to read, to go for a walk or for a massage are all extremely good for our well-being and that our well-being depends on how we look after ourselves, how kind and gentle we are with ourselves. But sometimes the gap between theory and putting things into practice is too big a jump. There is one more email we could be answering or something that we haven't quite finished.

But looking after ourselves and our well-being is not selfish. In fact, we often give others most of our attention throughout the day – our loved ones or our colleagues – but we are not prepared to give ourselves some time to simply 'BE' and to rest. When I run my Mindfulness workshops with students and staff, I remind everyone that we are called 'human beings' not 'human doings' so it is important to BE human from time to time.

The beauty of simply 'being' is that it brings a peaceful feeling that cannot be equalled. It is so easy to achieve yet so difficult in the sense that we often feel that we cannot stop thinking or engaging with a given situation. It doesn't take long and once you have developed the habit, it becomes easier and easier.

How is your mental/physical/social/ emotional/spiritual health doing?

So, as a member of staff in HE, what is your own level of stress and most importantly are you flourishing or languishing?

The Flourishing Model (FM) does not simply apply to students; it applies to staff too: it could be seen as a model for 'human flourishing' that can be used by all of us, ourselves included.

We know from research that if we are stressed out, our students will sense that stress and react accordingly. Students might not share how they are feeling or what's on their mind if they can see that we are overwhelmed or come across as stressed out.

A study published in *Nature Neuroscience*[46] shows that the neurons in the hippocampus of mice that had been exposed to stress, and those of their partner that didn't experience the stress but just observed it in their partner, changed in the same way. This has major implications and motivates us to really look at our own level of stress (as parents and lecturers, educators or teachers). In short, if we are stressed our children or the young people we teach will also adapt to that stress and might even adapt their brain structure in response. Even if further research needs to be done on this topic, it motivates us to take a more systemic approach to change as we clearly have influence in the system.

Your skills

Listening skills and empathy

Our students said that they have three major needs: to love, to be loved and to feel secure. This is something all human beings have in common. The students also said that they need to trust us and to know that we have their best interests at heart. This trust can best be developed by creating a relationship based on the Rogerian Core Conditions.

These conditions do not suggest that we never challenge our students. In fact, challenge is very much part of our work. But I believe that it can be done from the angle of the core conditions: empathy, unconditional positive regard and congruence.

Carl Rogers (1995, p.39) described empathy as:

the ability to perceive the internal frame of reference of another with accuracy, and with the emotional components and meanings which pertain thereto, as if one were the other person but without ever losing the 'as if' condition. Thus, it means to sense the hurt or the pleasure of another as he senses it, and to perceive the causes thereof as he perceives them, but without ever losing the recognition that it is as if I were hurt or pleased etc. If this 'as if' quality is lost, then the state is one of identification.

From experience I have noticed that empathy cannot really be achieved if we do not feel a connection to the person we are supporting or feel close to their situation. In short, depending on how we feel connected to others, our response may vary. Mindfulness can help us develop the skills to be empathic and good listeners: two of the skills students need from us when they are experiencing difficulties and want to share with us.

Research and its empirical evidence demonstrate that Mindfulness practice encourages the development of skills that impact on trainees' effectiveness as therapists. In a four-year qualitative study (Newsome et al. 2006; Schure et al. 2008), after taking a 15-week course that included Mindfulness meditation and counselling, students reported considerable positive effects on their counselling skills and therapeutic relationships, including being more attentive to the therapy process, more comfortable with silence and more attuned with themselves and clients.

Compassion and self-compassion

I know from speaking with both students and staff alike that some people do not like the word 'empathy' and prefer 'compassion' instead. When I learned Mindfulness, my teacher taught me that compassion is recognizing our human condition and acknowledging that it requires us to experience both positive and negative experiences. We all have good times and bad times. We all suffer. When we acknowledge that shared humanity, we feel more connected to others. Professor Neff has done a lot of work on compassion and most importantly on self-compassion. I would really recommend you go and explore her wonderful website.[47] Self-compassion could be the topic of a whole book. In fact, I give half-day and whole-day training courses on this topic but as a personal tutor and academic, however, I would really encourage you to take a few minutes to think about this concept of self-compassion – which is to give ourselves the same care and kindness we would give to one of our friends. When describing the Flourishing Model (FM), under cognitive health I mentioned mental chatter and our inner critic. I think these concepts apply to us as adults too. How often are we extremely critical with ourselves or harsh? How often do we minimize our own issues or make them bigger than they need to be?

Time

It is important to ensure that the conversations with students are not rushed so that students get a feeling that they're being heard and have a space to be heard. We all have a lot of work but it is vital that we remain present in the moment with students and that if students come to see us at a time when we are not free, we arrange a longer appointment later. At least two of the ten students I interviewed told me that it made a difference to them when they didn't feel like they were being a 'burden' and felt 'heard and understood' by their tutor. It might well be the first instance that a student expresses their feelings or talks about their emotions and this could make a big difference to them.

Confidentiality

Confidentiality is central to the creation of trust between students and members of staff. If we want students to discuss their issues and problems with us and also if we want to be able to help them, it is important that they feel that we are going to keep their information safe and confidential unless there is compelling evidence for us not to. Establish clear ground rules at the start which clearly deal with confidentiality and limits and follow the procedures set by your institution.

During our work, we come across a wide range of situations and events that happen to students. We may be tempted to discuss them with fellow colleagues but we need to remember that any information about identifiable students is confidential. It is vital to take great care to not disclose such information to friends, colleagues or family, unless they are directly involved in the teaching of the student and need to be informed. Universities have their own rules and regulations about confidentiality and it is important that to know, understand and respect these.

Know your limits – what to say, not to say

We are not health-care experts so it is extremely important that regardless of our impressions of services provided by GPs or other departments in our institutions, we do not give students any advice which could be detrimental to them.

I often have students who tell me that some tutors have said not to worry about the way they feel and that it may disappear. They have either advised them not to go to see a GP because they are likely to give them antidepressants or vice-versa that they should go and see their GP because they would be given something to help them with their condition. I feel that this could potentially be very damaging for the student's health and it also sets expectations and preconceptions which are not good for anyone. As academic tutors, we do not have the relevant training and experience to understand what medication would be beneficial or not for students. Most importantly, we do not have students' medical history and as a result cannot know what they need medically. It is therefore vital to refrain from sharing our beliefs around medication. As indicated previously, some students will clearly not require any medical treatment but others will; it is important to not make these decisions ourselves but to let qualified people do so instead.

Boundaries, boundaries, boundaries – do you know where to refer your students?

It may seem pretty obvious to most of us but it is vital to know what services are available within our department, school, faculty and institution overall.

Most institutions provide amazing pastoral services for students ranging from student health services, counselling services, vulnerable students' services, senior tutors or mental health advisers. They may have various names in various settings but what is vital for students is that members of staff know who the main points of contact are and can refer students confidently. So, how well do you know the services in your university? Do you know who to refer students to and how to 'escalate' if required? Would you be able to explain this clearly to your students?

Guiding rather than leading

Leading suggests that we are taking others in a specific direction and almost telling them where to go and what to do. In the case of students, it would mean leading them in a specific direction or giving them advice to do or not do something specific. It is sometimes tempting to give students specific instructions because we believe we have been in the same situation and have the answer for them. But in reality we are different individuals and our past experiences and knowledge might not be the best thing they need. From my conversations with students, it is clear that they understand how much they have been led during their secondary school studies.

Some students have said that they remember times when their tutors clearly tried to help them by giving them advice such as 'you need to go home and have a break', giving their opinion on their situation or telling them what to do. But they added that these comments, even though they seemed to be given because their tutor cared, did not help them at all. For them, it is better to be presented with options so that they can make an informed choice.

Guiding, on the other hand, is more about recognizing that the person in front of us knows where they want to go and what outcomes they want to achieve; our role is to guide and support them in getting there. If students don't know what they want or where they want to go, we can act as a navigation or support system to enable them to get to the best place possible based on some of the wants and needs they are expressing.

This means listening to the person who is experiencing difficulties in a respectful way – by being non-directive and paying attention. This will enable the student to express themselves freely so that they don't feel judged, directed or guided and, most importantly, without having to hear our comments, opinions or advice, nor our personal experiences that we decide to share with them 'because it might be of interest'. (But also because, let's be honest, there is a part of us that likes talking about ourselves but the fact is that students don't care!) To do this effectively, we need to be aware of our unconscious bias too.

The final aim is to try and give back control to students so that they feel empowered to take responsibility and choose how to deal with a specific situation and become independent and balanced individuals. For example, it is good to leave students with a clear plan and next steps, even if it means that you find out some information for them.

We may want to consider ourselves as coaches (sports or management) who are there to hold the space of our tutees to explore specific areas and topics, but we never give them the answer nor tell them what they should be doing or what they want to change. It's really for each individual to decide on these aspects.

Can you recognize what is going on with your tutees?

How much awareness do you have and can you recognize what is going on with your tutees?

As we have seen before, we cannot usually change the events in our own life but most importantly in others' lives. These events can include physical illness, a death or mental illness. The most challenging aspect is that we cannot act on the way our students are experiencing these stressful events. Every individual goes through life the way they want, depending on their personalities, their past (their roots) and their mental models, which are all linked to their education, social cultural environment, age, well-being, and so on.

This feeling of powerlessness can make us feel like we are unable to help. It might also make us want to avoid students who are experiencing difficulties because we feel uncomfortable. In our society where we are expected to act and to 'do things', it is difficult to simply be there and listen.

Do your students know that you are not indifferent to their suffering and that you really feel empathy for them?

When we don't know how to show that we care or are uncomfortable around students who are experiencing issues, it sends the message that we are trying to avoid the situation or distance ourselves from it. The student may get a sensation of being misunderstood or feeling lonely.

So, are you clear about your intentions when you help students? Having a clear intention is great but what matters is the result. It is important that as academic personal tutors and lecturers we think, observe and question what is going on so that we can become much more aware and conscious about focusing on the relationship we establish with our tutees. This means they feel we are truly listening, are interested in their situation and respectful of their differences and their experiences. It is sensible to adopt the principle that deep down we don't know this student nor do we fully understand what is happening; the best way to approach the situation is to be open-minded and present in the here and now.

How to bridge the student's skill gaps?

Conscious incompetence versus unconscious competence

There is a clear gap between our knowledge of a topic that students have chosen to study at university and their own knowledge. We are what I call 'unconsciously competent', whereas our students are 'consciously incompetent'. Let's have a look at this NLP concept and how it works.

It starts with unconscious incompetence – we don't know that we don't know. Let's use the example of driving a car to explain this further. Before we start taking driving lessons, we are not fully aware of all the skills required to drive a car. This is called unconscious incompetence. When we start having lessons, we become consciously aware of what we don't know – this is the second phase known as conscious incompetence. We realize that we need to think hard and to concentrate to change gears, use mirrors, turn, etc. As we become better drivers, we move on to conscious competence; this means that you 'know what you know' and are consciously aware of that knowledge. You can change gears or drive more easily but still need a lot of support from your instructor and need to focus on what you are doing. It might be that once you pass your driving test, you can drive the car on your own and are a 'conscious driver' with conscious competence but you would, for example, find it difficult to drive when a friend in the back of the car is chatting or with the radio on.

The final stage is unconscious competence – you don't know what you know. You do things almost automatically. At this point, as a driver you can drive miles on the motorway whilst thinking about some of your issues or what you are going to do when you get home or you can drive whilst listening to the radio, and so on.

As you can see from this example, there is a big gap and difference between conscious incompetence – you are aware of how much you don't know and understand yet – and unconscious competence where you know your topic and subject so well that you don't have to think very hard about it. Students arrive at university and usually find themselves in the conscious incompetence/conscious competence zone, whereas most of us are unconsciously competent. The problem in that situation is that interactions with students will be based on our beliefs that they also understand things and see things in the same way we do; we may not explain things in as much detail as they might require because we might believe that it is not necessary.

How to bridge the gap in knowledge

We need to first admit to ourselves that this is happening and acknowledge that whilst we are passionate, motivated and interested in a topic, and fully understand and know what we are talking about, our students arrive with completely different skills and knowledge. We also need to be empathetic, as we too were students once and didn't know as much as we do now.

It is therefore vital to bridge the gap between our knowledge so that students feel motivated and empowered to learn. One way to do so is to use scaffolding, which was first presented by Wood et al. in 1976. The theory is that when students are given the support they need whilst learning something new, they stand a better chance of using that knowledge independently.

Once we know students understand a concept or a theory, we can then take a step aside and let them work independently or in groups to apply these in context and strengthen and reinforce their knowledge.

Young people arrive from secondary school with the wing of knowledge truly developed because the current schooling system in England (as I've said several times – sorry to insist on this!) encourages rote learning for exams. However, the other wing, represented by other skills such as critical thinking, curiosity, openness and wisdom (to name but a few) which are the skills required by employers and companies in the 21st century, is not as developed. I often use the analogy of a bird with two wings that are not fully developed, which means that they cannot fly out of the nest and soar. At HE level, it is really important not to be tempted to simply reproduce this approach of teaching to test. Of course, it would be easier to do this as this is the model that young people have been exposed to for the majority of their schooling. But I strongly believe that adults need to help and support young people to develop themselves as whole individuals. I know this is a challenging aspect that requires us all (educators and young people alike) to step out of our comfort zones, but I think it is vital if we want well and flourishing students and young people.

Letting go of our own labels/bias – how do you define students' success?

How do you define students' success? How would you define someone who is successful and gets good grades at university? All these concepts have a great impact on how we interact with students and how they receive the information we provide them with.

It is extremely important for us to be aware of our unconscious bias: 'mental shortcuts based on social norms and stereotypes' (Guynn 2015). Biases can be based on skin colour, gender, age, height, weight, introversion versus extroversion, marital and parental status, disability status (for example, the use of a wheelchair or a cane), foreign accents, where someone went to college, and more (Wilkie 2014).

This universal tendency towards unconscious bias exists because bias is rooted in the brain. Scientists have determined that it is found in the same region of the brain (the amygdala) associated with fear and threat. But bias is also found in other areas of the brain. Stereotyping, a form of bias, is associated with the temporal and frontal lobes. The left temporal lobe of the brain stores general information about people and objects and is the storage place for social stereotypes. The frontal cortex is associated with forming impressions of others, empathy and reasoning (Henneman 2014).

In other words, our brain evolved to mentally group things together to help make sense of the world. The brain categorizes all the information it is bombarded with and tags that information with general descriptions it can quickly sort information into. Bias occurs when those categories are tagged with labels like 'good' or 'bad' and are then applied to entire groups. Unconscious bias can also be caused by conditional learning. For example, if a person has a bad experience with someone they categorize as belonging to a particular group, they often associate that entire group with that bad experience (Venosa 2015).

From a survival point of view, this mental grouping into good or bad helped the brain make quick decisions about what was safe or not safe and what was appropriate or not appropriate. It is a developed survival mechanism hardwired into our brains – and this makes it far more difficult to eliminate or minimize than originally thought (Ross 2008).

There is hope, however. One study found that hard-wired unconscious brain bias can be reversed. The study found that between 2006 and 2013, the implicit preference (or unconscious bias) for straight people over gays and lesbians declined by 13.4%. The author of the study acknowledged that whilst that percentage was significantly lower than the 26% decline in explicit preference (or expressed bias, if you will) during that same period, it showed that change can happen, albeit slowly, on an unconscious level (Jacobs 2015).

When we are unconsciously biased, we may tend to think everything about a person is good because we like that person or we form stereotypes and assumptions about certain groups that mean it's impossible to make an objective judgement about members of those groups. We may also seek information that confirms pre-existing beliefs or assumptions.

Price (n.d.) introduced the concept of group think, a bias that occurs when people try too hard to fit into a group by mimicking others or holding back thoughts and opinions. This causes them to lose part of their identities and causes organizations to lose out on creativity and innovation.

How we conceive our students or their abilities will therefore have an unconscious impact on how we behave and treat them. Having an understanding and knowledge that such biases occur is useful as it at least makes us consciously aware of them.

Chapter 6

The need for a systemic approach to change

'Is knowledge using you or are you using knowledge'
Don Miguel Ruiz Jr.

So far, we have talked about what you the tutor can do to support young people and to look after your own well-being. This book would not be complete if we didn't discuss the bigger picture and what can be done at the 'institution' level. This is what I would like us to do now in this chapter.

When I interviewed Professor Guy Claxton for the Flourishing podcast, he explained how our current schooling system encourages a DIKR approach – Direct instruction, knowledge rich. A deep knowledge is very important – after all, we want to make sure that a heart surgeon understands and knows what they are doing. However, like Professor Guy Claxton, I believe that when our education approach is too prescriptive, this can induce a potential lack of critical thinking. This can lead to the development of beliefs identified as 'THE truth' and a lack of open-mindedness essential for lifelong learning and development. When we believe in the existence of THE truth, this can make us believe that we are right. But is there even such a thing as THE truth? Perhaps what we have is OUR truth but not THE truth. Being open to other people's truth can help us grow and develop, and possibly even change our mind. This is exactly what's happened to me since March 2021 when I started having conversations on the podcast. They have enabled me to reconsider my views and thinking about education, and most importantly deepen my understanding. 128 (and counting) episodes later, I feel that every conversation has changed and reshaped me.

Knowledge or the belief that we know something inside out can also lead to a false sense of security that we've learned all that there is about a subject, that we know everything, have all the answers and there's nothing more to explore. In short, we can become really attached to our beliefs and knowledge and stop questioning or investigating other possible answers. In his book *The Five Levels of Attachment*,[48] Don Miguel Ruiz Jr states that humans have five potential levels of attachment: Authentic Self, Preference, Identity, Internalization and Fanaticism. He adds that at one end of the spectrum we are more connected to others and accepting; at the opposite end we are in total fear and believe we are right, have the answer and that everybody else is wrong.

This feeling that we know for sure and that the answer is at the back of a book, for example, jars against the uncertainty mentioned in a previous part of the book. It makes us less tolerant of uncertainty and to want an answer when sometimes it is not possible to get an answer. Covid is a good example.

Could it be that because we think we know for sure, we don't question our beliefs nor explore our mental models enough (if at all)? I will discuss this further when I discuss the iceberg model of Systems Thinking but for now, I'd like to invite you to pause for a minute, just long enough to ask yourself where you find yourself on the above continuum. Of course, for some topics you may only have preferences, whilst in other areas of your life you may be very attached to your views or knowledge. Reflecting on this can be very useful and might even start discussions and open up our thinking about topics in a more curious and open way. Why don't you take a few minutes to pause and think about this and give it a try?

Did Darwin get it wrong?

Most of us have heard about the theory expressed by Darwin that it's all about 'survival of the fittest' or 'dog eat dog'. But what if he didn't get it completely right? This is what evolution biologist and futurist Dr Elizabeth Sahtouris says and I think she might be on to something.[49] For her, Darwin was right about species competing for resources, but he didn't explore or go beyond this fact. Sahtouris's work shows that competition is just one stage in the maturation cycle. When we find ourselves at crisis point, we are forced to go beyond this competitiveness and find cooperative strategies for survival. Many crises are being talked about in our media – climate emergencies or the mental health crisis are two that come to mind straight away. Perhaps this is where as human beings we now find ourselves. We are at a crossroads and need to make a decision: carry on with our individualism and self-interest or take a different approach. Perhaps biology can help us understand this further.

Turning to biology for more insights

The biologists Francisco Varela and Humberto Maturana gave us the term 'autopoiesis' or self-creation or self-production, which explains why it is possible for a living entity to continually create itself and self-organize in relation to other entities.

In *The Ghost in the Machine* (1967), Arthur Koestler coined the phrase holarchy or a connection between holons. Holons are self-containing parts which are also part of a larger system. This means that we can be individuals who of course can display self-interest but also need to work in collaboration with the system we are part of, otherwise we will experience issues and might potentially destroy the overall system. One good way to explain this concept is by looking at our body as its own ecosystem; throughout the day it is a dynamic, self-sustaining system where trillions of cells collaborate to achieve allostasis – the process of maintaining homeostatis by adaptive internal change to the different demands imposed on the system (by the internal and external stress in the environment).

Sahtouris has long explained from her interest, love and observation of nature that there are clear phases in evolution.[50] Each cell starts with a state of unity or oneness and then separation or division occurs. This is then followed by hostile competition and often near extinction. In order to survive, negotiations follow, and cooperation prevails, giving rise to a higher level of unity and organization until the cycle begins again. This is part of what she calls the evolutionary process or maturation cycle.

For Sahtouris, human beings are relatively 'young' as a species compared to other older cells; as a result, we are mid-stage in our evolution and are still trapped like Darwin in competition and survival mode. We have already discussed the effects of being in survival mode (fight or flight) in Chapter 2 of the book so don't need to elaborate further, but we can now understand why languishing (or survival) created by constant competitiveness breeds perfectionism, fear of failure and imposter syndrome (based on *comparatitis* – this constant need to compare oneself to others).

If you want to understand this concept more, I would really recommend reading this fabulous article in *Health and Spirituality*.[51] As Sahtouris is quoted to say, 'we study rabbits in habitats but it's really all rabbitats.' We cannot separate human beings from their environments; but we can actually move to collaboration and cooperation instead. The exciting news is that we don't have to continue in the same way and it doesn't need to be a race with winners or losers. The process is never-ending. That's the principle of growth and evolution. It is emergent and is a generative process. We can rebalance with our nature and our environment.

Understanding what is going on in the world through adult developmental theory

As well as biology, we can have a look at psychology to deepen our understanding of what is going on. Kegan's adult developmental theory (1982, 1994)[52] can help us to gain a better understanding of how our growth does not stop after our teenage years; as adults we continue developing and experience changes to how we construct our reality. Kegan's work has been influenced by Piaget's work and his stages of cognitive development; Kegan states that there are five distinct developmental stages throughout our adult years. For him, becoming an adult is not simply about learning new things but about transformation. When I first encountered these, I felt they really fitted well with Sahtouris's work and the notion that we need to move to become more mature adults.

Here they are:[53]

- *Stage 1 – Impulsive mind (early childhood)*

This focuses on perception and impulse. Objects start to have a meaning for the child.

- *Stage 2 – Imperial mind (adolescence, 6% of adult population)*

In this stage, we are far more selfish and self-centred with a realization that we can act on our own desires. The underlying logic under that stage is 'what's in my best interest or it's all about me'.

- *Stage 3 – Socialized mind (58% of the adult population)*

Here we don't just look at others and situations as ways or obstacles to get our needs met but begin to internalize the values, expectations and beliefs around us from our society and family. We start to relate to others and become more part of society because society has become more part of us. We become a member of the tribe and focus on enhancing our relationships with others rather than on our own interests. This stage used to be perfectly adequate for our very traditional societies where there was a very simple way of how to live and what it meant to be a man or a woman in a tribe, when the rules were clear and simple. Nowadays though in a post-modern world with so many definitions of how we should live and who we should be and so many demands and complex problems to solve, the socialized mind becomes inadequate to the task. We can't simply be shaped by the environment. We need to develop an internal authority, compass or way that filters our reality, which leads us to the next level.

- *Stage 4 – Self-authoring mind (35% of the adult population)*

Most adults are expected to move to this stage. Typically, it begins in the 20s but for some it won't begin until their 40s. We can't just be written upon by our environment or culture. We don't simply take the environment in but need to pick up the psychological pen and author our own identity and set of beliefs. We become a more personal 'authority'. We remain a member of our community but can interrogate its rules and act on them. Kegan says that at the beginning when we object to the interpersonal arrangements that we have been part of or contracted to, this leads us to worry whether we will still be accepted, loved or will be excluded from our communities. This is the most dynamic and gradual transformation in our adult lives.

- *Stage 5 – Self-transforming mind (1% of the adult population)*

We come to the recognition that although our inner compass enables us to be powerful, inevitably our meaning-making system has limitations, blind spots, leaves something out, privileges some things and disadvantages other things. As we come to see those limits, we have the potential to step away from what we have been embedded in. That's the gradual move of development, where we move from being subject to a way of making meaning to being able to step back from it and turn that into an 'object'. It enables us to not just be a faithful abider of the law and someone who stands within an impressive system of law and society. We realize that these laws and our societies are imperfect. Up until now, we have for example excluded a certain group; we can reconstruct the system to include these people. We develop a humility that recognizes that there is room for improvement.

This transformation requires us to be psychologically safe enough so that we can leave our comfort zone and withstand the discomfort that will be part of the change process. With enough support, we can move away from the idea that the problem is not about the world but about us as individuals and the fact that we need to grow. This is done through facing challenges and problems that are difficult enough so that we can 'solve us'. If the challenge is big enough, it will create a desire to become a bigger version of ourselves and prevent us from falling back into our comfort zone. Kegan says that when a whole species is doing something, it's important to pay attention. Human beings are living longer and longer, enabling us to reach the higher states of human development which Kegan argues could be a potential way to solve the biggest problem of our survival. This makes a lot of sense to me and gives me a lot of hope. This idea of wisdom in our older years has been echoed by many of the Eastern philosophies, as well as ethnographers such as Gregory Bateson, Margaret Mead and most recently by Mary Catherine Bateson in her

book *Composing a Further Life: The Age of Active Wisdom*.[54]
She talks about a second stage of adulthood called Adulthood
II, which empowers us to redefine ourselves and challenge
ourselves to pursue new sources of meaning and ways to
contribute to society.

Beyond the mechanical view of our systems

Since researching mental health and well-being in education, I have noticed a dualistic approach to our problems:
the tendency to look at things as either black or white. We
also tend to treat our institutions or schools as an engine.
As a result, we are trying to tweak one part to make it work
(and even rev) better. So, for example, we focus on young
people's well-being mostly and sometimes solely. In this
approach, we don't realize or forget that our organizations
as whole ecosystems are dynamic and influenced by the
various parts that make them up. This creates unintentional
consequences and affects other parts in the system – staff
well-being. One example is how more staff members are
reporting higher levels of stress because they feel that their
workload has increased due to demands imposed on them
to ensure that students are happy and satisfied.

I also personally see an issue with a simple cause-and-
effect approach to solving complex issues such as mental
health. Whilst solution-focused approaches are extremely
useful for simple problems, I truly don't believe that these
work effectively for 'wicked problems', as presented by Rittel
and Webber in the 1970s. What might be more appropriate
is looking at complex topics through the lens of Systems
Thinking.

Your role – not in isolation but part of a whole

As I have just pointed out, in life there are two ways of looking at a situation. We can either choose simple cause-and-effect thinking, which suggests for example that university life is causing students to become more and more stressed, or we can choose to look at it from the lens of Systems Thinking.

Systems Thinking focuses on the whole system, looking at how the various parts of a system interact and through interrelated actions produce behaviours and lead to effects on each other. Senge (1990, p.7) defines it as 'a conceptual framework, a body of knowledge and tools that has been developed to make the full patterns clearer, and to help us see how to change them effectively'.

If we integrate this idea of Systems Thinking, we recognize that as members of staff we are both part of the problem and part of the solution. It encourages us to look at the issues experienced, try to understand how they have arisen and to gain more understanding and perspective to discover ways to deal with things differently.

In a video explaining what Systems Thinking is, Senge states that it is important for us to have a very deep and persistent commitment to 'learning' and we must be prepared to be wrong.[55] For him, if it is pretty obvious what we ought to be doing, then we would already be doing it. We are part of the problem – our own way of seeing things, our own sense of where there is leverage, is probably part of the problem too. Our 'mental models' are also an issue. If we are prepared to challenge our own mental models, we are more likely to find leverage and solutions. Finally, we need to triangulate and work collectively. We need to get different people, with different points of view and who are seeing different parts of the system, to come together and collectively start to see something that individually none of us can see.

This is extremely relevant in the case of the increased stress and anxiety reported by students. If we want to change things and find solutions, we need to work together (students, staff and all members of HE institutions).

The interviews I carried out with experts, students and members of staff have confirmed this aspect, making me even more convinced of the importance of the interaction between all the elements of an institution.

Interestingly, in a recent interview, Saul Kaplan explained that the reason we often keep developing targeted solutions is because we believe that our magic bullet of choice (new law, product, service or even more money) is going to be the perfect lever to completely transform the system.[56]

How to create a community instead of an 'institution' and allow student voices to be heard

During my conversations with students, they expressed the need for inclusion and for their voices to be heard. This is something that also regularly comes up in the National Student Survey (NSS). As we saw previously, Systems Thinking is the answer because it enables us to see our institution as a whole rather than as different parts (students, administrative and professional staff, academic members of staff, etc.) and to acknowledge that we all contribute to this whole system that is a HE institution, which generates the issues. It is therefore important for all of us to embrace the notion of the university as a garden where each one of us is a flower that will contribute to the overall beauty of the composition. It will also help us fully accept that we all have a role to play to ensure that changes happen; we have a garden which enables each individual flower to feel part of it but that is also allowed to fully bloom and fully be itself. Senge in *The Fifth Discipline* (1990) summarizes this when he says that 'Systems thinking shows us that there is no separate "other"; that you and the someone else are part of a single system. The cure lies in your relationship with your "enemy"' (p.67). When I read this, it really motivated me to connect with others in my institution to see how as a part of the system, I can contribute to improve the situation and create a positive environment for both staff and students to have a great experience.

We might want to start by looking at participation. In recent conversations on the podcast with young people, they told me how much they believe in the importance of youth-led initiatives. I completely agree with them. Young people need to be part of all conversations about change; it can't be token-istic. That said, if we look at Kegan's and Sahtouris's models, I personally don't think that youth-led initiatives are going to be enough. I recently interviewed Richard Fransham on the podcast. He is a Canadian advocate for change in education, particularly focused on youth agency (Episode 108). He told me that he doesn't think the youth-led adult supported initia-tive is ideal.

One suggestion he had was to use Hart's ladder of partic-ipation.[57] There are eight rungs in total: the bottom rung is manipulation, the second is decoration and the next one up is tokenism. The first three rungs represent no participation. Rung 4 is assigned but informed; rung 5 is consulted and informed. Rung 6 is adult-initiated, shared decisions with young people and it goes up to the top, which is basically co-creating. The seventh rung of is more like youth-led adult supported. What I love about the top rung is that age doesn't matter; it's about using the ideas to co-create together. Co-creation is maturation and fits in with Kegan's last level.

Using the Systems Thinking iceberg model to deepen our analysis

As explained previously, beyond very simple thinking we also have a tendency to react to individual problems that arise. I believe that this stems from the fact that we don't always look beyond the surface.

Using the Systems Thinking iceberg model will help you make sense of what I mean. It's well known that only 10% of the total mass of an iceberg is above the water, leaving 90% hidden and out of sight. What we don't consider is that the 90% can explain what we are seeing at the surface.

In the same way that we use the culture iceberg to understand our own or a foreign culture, so too can we use this to deepen our thinking about issues around mental health in education. The iceberg has four distinct levels.[58]

- At the top of the iceberg, visible above the water: the event – this is what we see in our daily lives and what we experience through our senses. 'What just happened?' can be used to find out more about the circumstances surrounding this event. This is where we react.
- At the second level are the patterns and trends that link the events through invisible threads. To find these out or anticipate these, we can ask ourselves

the following question: 'What trends or patterns have there been over time?'

- At the third level are the underlying systemic structures that explain the patterns. The questions we can use to discover these are: 'What has influenced the patterns?' 'What are the relationships between the parts?'

- Finally at the bottom are the most important parts – the mental models (we discussed these in the Flourishing Model or FM); they are part of the roots. In order to transform the system, we need to ask ourselves questions such as: 'What assumptions, beliefs and values do people hold about the system'? What beliefs keep the system in place?' The best way to become aware of these, according to Senge in *The Fifth Discipline*, is by 'personal mastery', which enables us to bring awareness by paying particular attention to our 'automatic thoughts'. Introducing mindfulness and self-awareness into our lives is a very powerful way to achieve this.

Interestingly, in the case of change in education, I don't often see open discussions about our mental models – why do we educate our young people in our schools the way we do? What are the different parts of the system and how do they influence the patterns and each other?

If we keep failing to ask and answer these questions, we will never truly be able to transform our education system. We need to broaden our perspective and look deeper. This of course requires all of us to take a good hard look at ourselves and to admit that for as long as we are part of the system, we influence it too. We are part of the problem but also part of the solution. Isn't that exciting!

At this point I would also like to introduce the work of Dr Ed Morrison and colleagues called *Strategic Doing – Ten Skills for Agile Leadership*, which might help us in our quest for change in education. In their book, they start by telling us that if we truly want to find answers to our wicked problems or challenges, we first need to shift from the traditional hierarchies which are truly representative of our great-grandparents or grandparents' economies and move to the creation of open, loosely connected networks (p.15) that come together because they have a particular task to complete which can best be achieve by all of them working together. These networks are the future and represent the economies of our grandchildren or great-grandchildren. We need to ensure that our young people have the skills to create such networks. Dr Morrison says that we first need to think differently about strategy because it is not something that can be done by an individual alone. It's a team sport. Morrison argues that 'the more complex the environment, the larger the group or network that will need to be engaged' (p.19). The size is very important but once again so is collaboration (and trust). Change cannot happen without those two ingredients. Morrison says that trust is 'established when words and actions align' (p.20).

We also need to start behaving differently – the suggestion here is to have high participation with high guidance. Everyone's voice is heard, but the discussion is guided and has direction.

Finally, we 'do' differently – this requires reading the book and applying the ten skills provided by the authors.

Strategic doing is an ongoing process of continuous doing and thinking which leads to learning by doing; although again there's no scope here to discuss this wonderful research further.[59] I would highly recommend reading the book by Dr Ed Morrison and colleagues so that you can find out more.

Now we've discussed the need for change, I'm going to share some potential ideals for a systemic approach.

Some examples of a more systemic approach

In this section, I would like to share with you two possible approaches to supporting change within a system. The first one is already in place and currently being explored by several HE institutions.

The University Mental Health Charter

This was created by Student Minds together with leading HE organizations and, most importantly, thousands of staff and students to shape the future in which everyone in HE can thrive.[60] It promotes a whole-university approach and offers a Mental Health Charter framework authored by Hughes and Spanner (2019), which provides a set of evidence-informed principles to support universities to adopt a whole-university approach to mental health and well-being. You can download a PDF version to find out more.[61] To get awarded the Charter, institutions sign up to be part of the voluntary accreditation scheme, which then brings together universities and Charter assessment teams. To me, this is a really wonderful (and much-needed) initiative. I think it is great to see a whole-university approach that promotes the well-being of students *and* staff, which fits in with what I have been saying during all my presentations and keynotes. We cannot have a flourishing education without flourishing students *and* flourishing staff.

I very much look forward to seeing how this unfolds, how many institutions take part in the scheme and, most importantly, what difference it makes in the long run to the daily lives of students and staff.

That said, I also believe it is extremely important for any process of change to address the deeper questions we mentioned previously in the iceberg model. I am convinced that the current hierarchical top-down approach is not enough. If we want systemic change in our institutions, we need to consider every member of the organization and community. In doing so, we will foster an engagement, a real wanting to contribute and be part of the movement.

For this reason, I would now like to introduce a second approach for change, which can be used not just by universities and HE institutions but by all educational settings, if they so wish.

What I particularly love about this model is that it enables organizations to get to know and understand their own culture and look at their iceberg in order to decide on specific changes required. To do this, I interviewed my friend Louise Wiles,[62] Change and Transition Coach and Consultant, who uses Appreciate Inquiry in her work and trained with the Wellbeing Lab.[63]

Appreciative Inquiry

In her work, Louise uses an alternative framework for thinking about well-being, Dr McQuaid's model drawing on Professor Seligman's PERMA model,[64] which stands for positive emotion, engagement, positive relationships, meaning, accomplishment or achievements, to which Dr McQuaid added H for health.[65] Well-being is defined using Professor Huppert et al.'s (2013) work: 'An ability to feel good and function effectively and navigate the highs and lows of life' (p.837).

It's not about feeling fantastic or functioning brilliantly but 'well and good', which echoes Winnicott's concept of the 'good-enough' parent.[66]

With individuals, Louise reviews the PERMAH survey as a way of helping people to identify ways in which they can generate higher levels of well-being.[67] She comes from a position of positivity and possibility rather than a point of deficit. Rather than asking questions that focus on the problem or challenge and delving into its causes, the process is based on the belief that a positive situation and framework is much more powerful.

This book has been about creating a flourishing education system. Imagine if we held this as a vision for the creation of a flourishing system of education that could emerge from and through processes of change that prioritize vitality and well-being and is founded on the assumption that every organizational system possesses strengths, which when identified and harnessed provide a positive source of energy that enables both individual and organizational transformation. Appreciative Inquiry (AI) provides an excellent approach for institutions, organizations and communities to create positive disruption that supports systemic flourishing, founded on a process of curiosity; innovation and experimentation.[68]

AI was first designed as an action research methodology by David Cooperrider (1986). Here we will use the six stages identified and developed by Dr McQuaid and Dr Cooperrider in their book *Your Change Blueprint*.[69]

The AI process has six stages:

Define
Discover
Dream
Design
Destiny
Drum

Define

It is important to begin with an intentional topic as human systems all move in the direction of what is persistently talked and asked about. In the design stage we ask appreciative and generative questions such as: 'What do we want to grow or advance?' 'What do we most want to create around this area of focus?' A suggestion for the area of flourishing education could be: Empowering all stakeholders to become flourishing lifelong learners.

Discover

This stage is about uncovering the strengths in the system by asking appreciative questions about the best of what is and what has been. These questions are designed to identify what is and has been working well. It's about bringing hope and optimism into the process and building confidence by recognizing the strengths and resources already in existence in the system or the situation.

We know from neuroscience and work by Barbara Fredrickson[70] and her Broaden and Build theory that we are a lot more creative when we think from a positive and open frame of mind than when we are talking about what is wrong or challenging.

Dream

In this stage we uncover possibilities and ask 'what might be possible'. The aim here is to surface hopes and build on strengths as people across the system think about what positive progress, achievements, breakthroughs and end results could be. 'Big bold, creative images of the future are explored', according to Dr McQuaid.[71] The aim is to develop vivid images of the future that they want to create, an image that will propel people forward.

Design

This is where thoughts begin to converge towards eventual plans for action. In this phase, participants brainstorm and build pathways towards creating their future, asking how they might get there. The aim is to create multiple pathways that inspire and energize people towards the desired change. The pathways created could be around organizational culture and purpose, partnerships, educational offerings, or approaches to learning and strategies.

Deploy/Destiny

This next stage is all about people taking responsibility and beginning to take action to bring the pathways to life and achieve what they hope to achieve. The question is where to start as people are encouraged to find their ways forward and create the change that has been imagined.

Drum

The final D in this six-stage process stands for drum (McQuaid 2018). This draws on research that found that it is what happens after the AI process and conversation that really makes the difference. Change requires a reiterative process to keep the dream alive and the supportive environment created by the AI process.

Are all systems ready to embark on a process of AI? If there are a lot of dysfunctions and not much openness or opportunity for people to speak up in a psychologically safe environment, then this needs to be addressed and given space before the AI summit or process begins.

Interestingly, when I spoke to my colleague and researcher Natalie Rothwell-Warn, who is using AI in her current education doctorate (EdD) work, she told me that something important happened when participants shared their stories and circumstances. Natalie said the space created generates a safe space, a research space where the UN Convention on the Right of the Child (UNCRC) and confidentiality prevails. It also enables the participants to reflect deeply and many have commented saying: '*wow, nobody has asked me what I think before.*' Or '*no one has sat me down, given me the time or the space to open up.*'

In a way, Natalie says, this is where AI allows for the negative to come through (or at least she has as a researcher) because it's only from coming out, finding their voices and being allowed to speak up that the participants can move forward and say 'that's how I'd like it to change'. AI and David Cooperrider would probably insist that because it is a very positive approach, you only take the positive that is going on in the institution and only use the best examples that you can build on. Natalie, however, argues that before we can do this, we need to allow whatever negativity to come out because we are dealing with people's real experiences which we need to listen to if we are to achieve genuine authentic transformation. When we allow this to happen, the participants feel able to talk about what their dream is and how they would envision a flourishing education system. When we know what we don't want, we can then talk about what we want instead. Natalie says that this is an opportunity to acknowledge where the participants are and a way to say: 'it's OK to be where you are, it's OK to feel as you do and here's the space to let it all out.' So before we focus on only the positives, we give space, allow time and acknowledge whatever pain and negative to come out first. We can then ask – now we know what's not working, let's flip it – what would you like instead? Are there any aspects in the organization where this is already happening? What has contributed to it?

I really like this approach as I know from talking to staff members and students in HE settings that they don't always feel like they can share. I truly believe that if we could organize events that enable this process, we would see real change in our organizations. The beauty of AI is that it can take any format – from individual coaching conversations to small-scale workshops to a massive summit with hundreds of participants.

For this change to happen, there is one last concept that Louise mentioned that I need to introduce: the 'Me, We, Us' model created by Aaron Jarden, Senior Lecturer at Auckland University of Technology.[72]

- The Me considers change at the individual level;
- We at the group level (School or Faculty); and

- Us at the institution level.

'Me' interventions are all the suggestions I have made when describing the Flourishing Model (FM). They don't need the interventions of others to happen.

'We' interventions relate to what we can do with our line managers, or our own team if we are a line manager ourselves. I would argue that it also includes students at all levels. Jarden suggests strategies and tasks such as job crafting (Wrzesniewski 2014) or building high-quality connections (Dutton and Heaphy 2003).

Finally, 'Us' interventions are initiatives such as the 'Mental Health Charter' mentioned in the previous section, which require the whole of the organization to be involved, including all employees (and all students). Another example would be the well-being resources made available for everyone in an institution or even an AI summit, as suggested by Cooperrider and Whitney (2005).

According to Louise, there is a much greater interaction perspective at the 'we' and 'us' level. It is not just the fact that we think about well-being at the relationship level; it is more that we are interacting and impacting others constantly, whether we are thinking about it or not. This impacts their and our well-being, the same at the organizational level. A policy may be institution wide, but it has impacts beyond the institution to the local community, other stakeholders including parents, relatives, and so on – and their reaction feeds back to the institution.

I think AI is a very promising and exciting process and method which provides us with an opportunity to truly get all stakeholders to discuss what change around well-being in education might look like. It allows participants to identify a keystone change based on shared values, a shared language and vision. Over time we can establish trust and safe spaces, which are the key ingredients for any change to happen.

What next?

> *'A journey of a thousand miles begins*
> *with a single step' – Lao Tzu*

When I started this journey and my research into mental health, resilience and well-being in HE, I really didn't expect to end with this book and the Flourishing Model (FM). At the start of my one-year career break in September 2021, I never anticipated that I would be writing a second edition of this book. Writing this book has definitely been a journey of a thousand miles and every day, every week has meant taking a step towards something new. It has enabled me to 'test out' my own model (sometimes to the limit) and to see for myself how much any imbalances between my cognitive, physical, emotional, spiritual and social health have an impact on my own ability to flourish.

It certainly has taught me that I have a choice and that I am responsible for the outcomes in my life. Most importantly, it has taught me that if I want to give my students advice, I also need to look after my own well-being and make choices so that I can be an example to others and bring out the best in students and the belief that they cannot only enjoy but also flourish at university. Gandhi said that 'You must be the change you wish to see in the world.' This is what I am trying to achieve with this book and with what I do daily. My only hope is that reading this book will have the same effect on you. The conversations I had with students and with experts and colleagues have enabled me to create the model in this book and showed me that there are vital elements to flourishing.

Understanding

This means understanding what is going on in our lives, the differences between languishing and flourishing and between mental health and mental disorders (and what lies in between). But also understanding that our mental health is closely linked to our social, physical, emotional and spiritual health and that we need to look at ourselves and others holistically. Happiness is definitely an inside job but isn't permanent. There will be challenging times and moments which are more difficult (ups and downs). Happiness is a journey not a destination. Mental health (and all the others) is on a continuum. We cannot always be flourishing or always languishing; depending on the situations in our lives, we go up and down the scale. Without a clear understanding of who we are, what we stand for and how this ecosystem (body with trillions of cells) reacts to situations, there is no way to fully flourish.

Awareness

When we develop awareness, we become aware of our thoughts, emotions, feelings and sensations and can accept and welcome them in our lives rather than fighting or trying to control them. When we acknowledge what is happening in our lives without judgement, we can then focus on finding a suitable solution. All of us currently spend so much time on our phones and screens. What would happen if we spent even half of that time getting to know ourselves, being present and noticing what is going on for us on a daily basis instead?

A toolbox

Just like a plumber or an electrician has a toolbox for his or her work, it is extremely important to create our own toolbox of resources to help us in life. I'm hoping that you will be able to practise some of the exercises in the book and keep them in your toolbox for resilience and well-being, not just for yourself but also to share with other colleagues and your tutees and students.

The Flourishing Model (FM) was created based on the conversations I had with experts in the UK, Canada and the US, but most importantly by interviewing 33 students based at various UK universities. The next step is to try and carry out the AI process in different settings and see what happens when we create a safe space and trust. Can we effect positive change in education?

Designing and building positive institutions as change agents for a better world

As we have seen in the previous sections, it's not a question of simply asking our staff and students to look after their well-being or to get to know what type of flower or plant they are and how they contribute to their ecosystem. Some organizations may ask for or suggest specific training so that individuals can become more resilient. This is totally possible and achievable. The only issue with this approach is that when these more resilient individuals return to a dysfunctional environment which does not foster well-being, it can lead to two things: a real sense of hopelessness (and helplessness), which we know from Seligman and Maier's research is highly connected to depression (1967), or it will make the individual realize that the environment is not 'for them', that it is not taking care of their needs and so they leave. Either way, that's a negative outcome as it means not only unhappy staff and students, but becomes a real retention issue with a loss of talent and pool of amazing contributors to our organizations. The best way to approach change in education is by trying to introduce a more systemic approach, as mentioned in this chapter. We can achieve true flourishing in our organizations (and as a result in our individual lives) when we can bring everybody together to build a better world; and when we are able to experience what Cooperrider and Fry (2012) call 'mirror flourishing', which is the growing together that happens naturally and reciprocally when we actively engage or witness the acts that help nature, others or the world as a whole to flourish.

This requires us to move from the 'fear-based approach'. Instead of focusing on the individual who needs to compete with others to win or to stay alive, thus triggering our fight, flight or worse our freeze response, we shift to a more 'love-based approach', which requires us to recognize that we are social animals who need to feel connected to others, to collaborate and cooperate to be well and live well. It is possible to unwind our nervous system over time by moving away from the stress response to settle into our natural state of being present, in harmony with what is. It's a continuous process which is generative and never-ending. Some days we will do better than others. As we have seen in this book, we are not victims of our genes, emotions or thoughts. We can choose, and that choice enables us to consciously engage our social engagement system or ventral vagal system. I believe the 'love-based' approach is truly the right name for it since this system recruits our hearts. It requires us to be in the present moment, and leads us to feeling more grounded, calmer, curious, open and compassionate. Over the last few years, I have been developing this 'love approach' and taking humble steps in this direction. I am like a lighthouse standing by the harbour of change in education to welcome anybody interested in and wanting to join me on this fabulous journey to true collaboration. Are you ready? I can't wait for us to connect.

From one colleague to another

Now that you have read this book and discovered this model, you may ask yourself how you can share your ideas or even get further training, including in Mindfulness.

I believe it's extremely useful to discuss and share experiences and challenges with other colleagues. It's both inspiring and motivating to discuss strategies and solutions with individuals from different institutions.

All the activities in this book have been shared with you to get you to test them out and practise them on your own. Please feel free to email to share your thoughts and views with me too.

Sharing with others

Einstein stated that '*If you can't explain* it simply, *you don't understand* it well enough.' I believe that the more we share and discuss the ideas contained in this book, the better and easier it will be to apply and use them in our daily lives. Mindfulness is not simply a tool; it is a way of life. It is something that becomes engrained and habitual; we do not think about it but use it naturally and regularly. This comes with time, patience and practice. We never get there... life is a journey and so there isn't a final destination.

If you would like to share your experience with others, feel free to connect with me on LinkedIn,[73] Twitter,[74] Instagram or to join our Facebook page – Flourishing Education.[75] This is a safe and supportive group where you can discuss the various methods, ask questions and share what worked well (or not so well) for you with other like-minded individuals.

For more information on workshops, events and training courses from the author of this book, check out www.flourishingeducation.co.uk.

Wishing you well on your journey to flourishing...

References

Adler, P.S. 'The transitional experience: An alternative view of culture shock' in *Journal of Humanistic Psychology*, 15 (4), 13–23 (1975).

American Psychiatric Association. *Diagnostic and statistical manual of mental disorders*, 5th ed. Washington, DC (2013).

Andrews, B. and Wilding, J.M. 'The relation of depression and anxiety to life-stress and achievement in students' in *British Journal of Psychology*, 95, 509–521 (2004).

Bandler, R. and Grinder, J. *The structure of magic I.* Paolo Alto, CA: Science and Behavior Books (1975).

Banks, S. *The missing link*. Vancouver: Lone Pine (1998).

Benard, B. *Fostering resiliency in kids: Protective factors in the family, school, and community*. Portland, OR: Western Center for Drug-Free Schools and Communities (1991).

Benard, B. *Resiliency: What we have learned*. Oakland, CA: WestEd (2004).

Bennett, T.H. and Holloway, K.R. 'Drug misuse among university students in the UK: Implications for prevention' in *Substance Use & Misuse*, 49 (4), 448–455 (2013).

Bernstein, A. *The myth of stress: Where stress really comes from and how to live a happier and healthier life.* New York: Atria Books (2010).

Bierwisch, M. 'Some semantic universals of German adjectivals' in *Foundations of Language*, 3, 1–36 (1967).

Bohm, D. *Thought as a system.* Abingdon: Routledge (1994).

Boucher, J. and Osgood, C.E. 'The Pollyanna hypothesis' in *Journal of Verbal Learning and Verbal Behavior*, 8, 1–8 (1969).

Braden, G. *Fractal time: The secret of 2012 and a new world age.* New York: Hay House (2012).

Bronfenbrenner, U. 'Toward an experimental ecology of human development' in *American Psychologist*, 32 (7), 513–531 (1977). https://doi.org/10.1037/0003-066X.32.7.513

Cacioppo, J.T., Crites, S.L., Jr., Gardner, W.L. and Berntson, G.G. 'Bioelectrical echoes from evaluative categorizations: I. A late positive brain potential that varies as a function of trait negativity and extremity' in *Journal of Personality and Social Psychology*, 67, 115–125 (1994).

Cacioppo, J.T., Gardner, W.L. and Berntson, G.G. 'Beyond bipolar conceptualizations and measures: The case of attitudes and evaluative space' in *Personality and Social Psychology Review*, 1, 3–25 (1997).

Canfield, J. *The success principles: How to get from where you are to where you want to be.* New York: William Morrow Paperbacks; reprint edition (2006).

Cannon, W.B. *Bodily changes in pain, hunger, fear and rage: An account of recent researches into the function of emotional excitement.* New York and London: D. Appleton and Co. (1915).

Cannon, W.B. *Bodily changes in pain, hunger, fear, and rage,* 2nd ed. New York: Appleton-Century-Crofts (1929).

Cannon, W.B. *Wisdom of the body.* London: W.W. Norton & Company (1932).

Cao, W., Fang, Z., Hou, G., Han, M., Xu, X., Dong, J. and Zheng, J. 'The psychological impact of the COVID-19 epidemic on college students in China' in *Psychiatry Research,* 287, Article 112984 (2020). https://doi.org/10.1016/j.psychres.2020.112934

Carleton, R.N. 'Into the unknown: A review and synthesis of contemporary models involving uncertainty' in *Journal of Anxiety Disorders,* 39, 30–43 (2016).

Chambers, R., Gullone, E. and Allen, N.B. 'Mindful emotion regulation: An integrative review' in *Clinical Psychology Review,* 29, 560–572 (2009).

Chamorro-Premuzic, T. and Furnham, A. 'Personality predicts academic performance: Evidence from two longitudinal university samples' in *Journal of Research in Personality,* 37, 319–338 (2003a).

Chamorro-Premuzic, T. and Furnham, A. 'Personality traits and academic examination performance' in *European Journal of Personality,* 17, 237–250 (2003b).

Chomsky, N. *Current issues in linguistic theory.* The Hague: Mouton (1964).

Cicero, M.T. *Selected works,* translated by Michael Grant. New York: Penguin; New Impression edition (1974).

Cline, F.W. and Fay, J. *Parenting with love and logic: Teaching children responsibility.* Colorado Springs, CO: Pinon Press (1990).

Cooperrider, D. *Appreciative Inquiry: Toward a methodology for understanding and enhancing organisational innovation.* Ph.D. dissertation (1986).

Cooperrider, D. and Whitney, D. *Appreciative Inquiry: A positive revolution in change.* San Francisco, CA: Berrett-Koehler Publishers (2005).

Cooperrider, D. and Fry, R. 'Mirror flourishing and the positive psychology of sustainability+' in *Journal of Corporate Citizenship*, 46, 3–12. (2012). https://doi-org.bris.idm.oclc.org/10.9774/GLEAF.4700.2012.su.00002

Corcoran, K.M., Farb, N., Anderson, A. and Segal, Z.V. 'Mindfulness and emotion regulation: Outcomes and possible mediating mechanisms' in A.M. Kring and D.M. Sloan (eds), *Emotion regulation and psychopathology: A transdiagnostic approach to etiology and treatment,* pp. 339–335. New York: Guilford Press (2010).

Coué, E. *Self mastery through conscious autosuggestion.* London (1922).

Coué, E. *How to practice suggestion and autosuggestion*. New York: American Library Service (1923).

Dalai Lama and Cutler, H.C. *The art of happiness: A handbook for living*, 1st ed. London: Hodder & Stoughton (1999).

Deci, E.L. and Ryan, R.M. 'The "what" and "why" of goal pursuits: Human needs and the self-determination of behaviour' in *Psychological Inquiry*, 11, 227–268 (2000).

Deci, E.L., and Ryan, R.M. (2008). 'Hedonia, eudaimonia and well-being: An introduction' in *Journal of Happiness Studies*, 9, 1–11 (2008).

Dinan, T.G. and Cryan, J.F. 'The impact of gut microbiota on brain and behaviour: Implications for psychiatry' in *Current Opinions, Clinical Nutrition and Metabolic Care*, 18 (6), 552–558 (2015).

Dodge, R., Daly, A., Huyton, J. and Sanders, L. 'The challenge of defining wellbeing' in *International Journal of Wellbeing* [online], 2 (3), 222–235 (2012).

Dunn, J.R. and Schweitzer, M.E. 'Feeling and believing: The influence of emotion on trust' in *Journal of Personality and Social Psychology*, 88, 736–748 (2005).

Dutton, J. and Heaphy, E. 'The power of high quality connections' in K. Cameron, J. Dutton and R. Quinn (eds), *Positive organizational scholarship: Foundations of a new discipline*, pp. 263–278. San Francisco, CA: Berrett-Koehler (2003).

Dweck, C. *Mindset: The new psychology of success.* New York: Ballantine Books (2007).

Egan, R., MacLeod, R., Jaye, C., McGee, R., Baxter, J. and Herbison, P. 'What is spirituality? Evidence from a New Zealand hospice study' in *Mortality*, 16 (4), 307–324 (2011).

Emmons, R.A. and McCullough, M.E. 'Counting blessings versus burdens: An experimental investigation of gratitude and subjective well-being in daily life' in *Journal of Personality and Social Psychology*, 84, 377–389 (2003).

Farb, N.A.S., Segal, Z.C., Mayberg, H., Bean, J., McKeon, D., Fatima, Z. and Anderson, A.K. 'Attending to the present: Mindfulness meditation reveals distinct neural modes of self-reference' in *Social Cognitive and Affective Neuroscience*, 2, 313–322 (2007).

Fredrickson, B.L., Mancuso, R.A., Branigan, C. and Tugade, M.M. 'The undoing effect of positive emotions', in *Motivation and Emotion*, 24 (4), 237–258 (2000). https://doi.org/10.1023/a:1010796329158

Fromm, E. *The sane society.* Abingdon: Routledge Classics (2001).

Fromm-Reichmann, F. 'Loneliness' in *Psychiatry: Journal for the Study of Interpersonal Processes*, 22, 1–15 (1959).

Gunaratana, H. *Mindfulness in plain English.* Somerville, MA: Wisdom Publications (2002).

Guynn, J. 'Google's "bias busting" workshops target hidden prejudices' in *USA Today* (12 May 2015). Available from: www.usatoday.com/story/tech/2015/05/12/google-unconsciousbias-diversity/27055485/ [accessed 6 September 2016].

Haidt, J. *The happiness hypothesis: Putting ancient wisdom and philosophy to the test of modern science.* London: Arrow Books (2006).

Hebert, E.A. and Dugas, M.J. 'Behavioral experiments for intolerance of uncertainty: Challenging the unknown in the treatment of generalized anxiety disorder' in *Cognitive and Behavioral Practice*, 26 (2), 421–436 (2019).

Henneman, T. 'You, biased? No, it's your brain'. Workforce (2014). Available from: www.workforce.com/articles/20242-you-biased-no-its-your-brain [accessed 6 September 2016].

Hoffman, S.G., Sawyer, A.T., Witt, A.A. and Oh, D. 'The effect of mindfulness-based therapy on anxiety and depression: A metaanalytic review' in *Journal of Consulting and Clinical Psychology*, 78, 169–183 (2010).

Hughes, G. 'Transition distress: The big problem facing universities' in *Human Givens Journal*, 19, 42–44 (2012).

Hughes, G. and Spanner, L. *The university mental health charter.* Leeds: Student Minds (2019).

Huppert, F.A. and So, T.T. 'Flourishing across Europe: Application of a new conceptual framework for defining wellbeing' in *Social Indicators Research*, 110 (3), 837–861 (2013).

Hyman, I. 'The dangers of going on autopilot' in *Psychology Today* (2014). Available from www.psychologytoday.com/blog/mental-mishaps/201404/the-dangers-going-autopilot [accessed 15 June 2016].

Hyman, I.E. Jr., Sarb, B.A. and Wise-Swanson, B.M. 'Failure to see money on a tree: Inattentional blindness for objects that guided behavior' in *Frontiers in Psychology* (23 April 2014). https://doi.org/10.3389/fpsyg.2014.00356

Ivtzan, I., Hefferon, K. and Worth, P. *Second wave positive psychology: Embracing the dark side of life*. Abingdon: Routledge (2015).

Jacobs, T. 'Anti-gay bias is even diminishing on an unconscious level' in *Pacific Standard*. (2015) Available from: www.psmag.com/health-and-behavior/anti-gay-bias-is-evendiminishing-on-an-unconscious-level [accessed 6 September 2016].

Jing-Schmidt, Z. 'Negativity bias in language: A cognitive affective model of emotive intensifiers' in *Cognitive Linguistics*, 18, 417–433 (2007) https://doi.org/10.1515/COG.2007.023

Joseph, J. *The resilient child*. New York: Insight Books (1994).

Kabat-Zinn, J. *Wherever you go, there you are: Mindfulness meditation in everyday life*. New York: Hyperion (1994).

Kadam, S. and Kotate, P.A. 'Theoretical perspective of the effects of assumptions on emotional well-being of an individual' in *International Journal of Indian Psychology*, 3 (4), 75 (2016).

Kegan, R. *The evolving self: Problem and process in human development*. Cambridge, MA: Harvard University Press (1982).

Kegan, R. *In over our heads: The mental demands of modern life*. Cambridge, MA: Harvard University Press (1994).

Keller, A., Litzelman, K., Eisk, L.E., Maddox, T., Cheung, E.R., Creswell, P.D., et al. 'Does the perception that stress affects health matter? The association with health and mortality' in *Health Psychology*, 31, 677–681 (2012).

Keyes, C.L.M. 'The mental health continuum: From languishing to flourishing in life' in *Journal of Health and Social Behavior*, 43, 207–222 (2002).

Keyes, C.L.M., Shmotkin, D. and Ryff, C.D. 'Optimizing well-being: The empirical encounter of two traditions' in *Journal of Personality and Social Psychology*, 82 (6), 1007–1022. (2002) https://doi.org/10.1037/0022-3514.82.6.1007

Keyes, C.L.M. 'Complete mental health: An agenda for the 21st century' in C.L.M. Keyes and J. Haidt (eds), *Flourishing: Positive psychology and the life well-lived*, pp. 293–312. Washington, DC: American Psychological Association (2003).

Killingsworth, M.A. and Gilbert, D.T. 'A wandering mind is an unhappy mind' in *Science*, 330 (6006), 932 (2010).

Kingsbury, E. 'The relationship between empathy and mindfulness: Understanding the role of self-compassion' in *Dissertation Abstracts International: Section B: Science and Engineering*, 70 (3175) (2009).

Korzybski, A. *Science and sanity: An introduction to non-Aristotelian systems and general semantics*, 5th ed. Fort Worth, TX: Institute of General Semantics (1933/1995).

Kreitz, C., Furley, P., Memmert, D. and Simons, D.J. 'Inattentional blindness and individual differences in cognitive abilities' in *PLoS ONE*, 10 (8), e0134675 (2015).

Lao, T. *Lao-Tzu's Taoteching*, translated by Porter, Bill (Red Pine), 3rd revised ed. Port Townsend, WA: Copper Canyon Press (2009).

Larcombe, W., Baik, C., Brooker, A., Wyn, J., Allen, L., Field, R. and James, R. (2017). *Enhancing student mental wellbeing*. Melbourne Centre for the Study of Higher Education. Available from http://melbourne-cshe.unimelb.edu.au/data/assets/pdf_file/0006/2408604/MCSHE-StudentWellbeing-Handbook-FINAL.pdf [accessed 3 October 2021].

LeDoux, J. *The emotional brain*. London: Orion Books (1998).

Leitch, L. 'The nervous system and resilience'. Threshold GlobalWorks (2015). Available from: www.thresholdglobalworks.com/pdfs/nervous-system-and-resilience.pdf [accessed 11 September 2016].

Lifton, R.J. *The protean self: Human resilience in an age of transformation*. New York: Basic Books (1993).

Locke, J., Campbell, M.A. and Kavanagh, D.J. 'Can a parent do too much for their child? An examination by parenting professionals of the concept of overparenting' in *Australian Journal of Guidance and Counselling*, 22(2), 249–265 (2012).

Loehr, J. and Schwartz, T. *The power of full engagement: Managing energy, not time, is the key to high performance and personal renewal.* New York: Free Press (2005).

Macmin, L. and Foskett, J. "'Don't be afraid to tell." The spiritual and religious experience of mental health service users in Somerset' in *Mental Health, Religion & Culture*, 7 (1), 23–40 (2004).

Mandler, G. 'Presidential address to Division 1 (General Psychology) of the American Psychological Association. Consciousness: Its function and construction'. Centre for Human Information Processing, University of California at San Diego, June 1983.

McCrae, R.R. and Costa, P.T. 'Validation of the five-factor model of personality across instruments and observers' in *Journal of Personality and Social Psychology*, 52(1), 81–90 (1987).

McMahan, E.A. and Estes, D. (2011). 'Hedonic versus eudaimonic conceptions of well-being: Evidence of differential associations with self-reported well-being' in *Social Indicators Research*, 103 (1). http://dx.doi.org/10.1007/s11205-010-9698-0

McQuaid, M. and Cooperrider, D. *Your change blueprint: How to design and deliver an AI summit*, 1st ed. Albert Park, Australia: Michelle McQuaid Pty Ltd (2018).

McWilliams, P. *Do it! Let's get off our buts.* Nashville, TN: Prelude Press (1994).

Moore, A. and Malinowski, P. 'Meditation, mindfulness and cognitive flexibility' in *Consciousness and Cognition*, 18, 176–186 (2009).

Munich, R.L. and Munich, M.A. 'Overparenting and the narcissistic pursuit of attachment' in *Psychiatric Annals*, 39, 227–235 (2009).

Neff, L.A. and Karney, B.R. 'Stress and reactivity to daily relationship experiences: How stress hinders adaptive processes in marriage' in *Journal of Personality and Social Psychology*, 97 (3), 435–450 (2009).

Newberg, A. and Waldman, M.R. *Words can change your brain: 12 conversation strategies to build trust, resolve conflict, and increase intimacy.* New York: Penguin; Illustrated edition (2014).

Newsome, S., Christopher, J.C., Dahlen, P. and Christopher, S. 'Teaching counselors self-care through mindfulness practices' in *Teachers College Record*, 108, 1881–1990 (2006).

Nietzsche, F. *Twilight of the idols* (R. Polt, trans.). Indianapolis, IN: Hackett (1997/1889).

Oberg, K. 'Culture shock: Adjustment to new cultural environments' in *Practical Anthropology*, 7, 177–182 (1960).

Ortner, C.N.M., Kilner, S.J. and Zelazo, P.D. 'Mindfulness meditation and reduced emotional interference on a cognitive task' in *Motivation and Emotion*, 31, 271–283 (2007).

Orwell, G. 'Politics and the English language' in *Horizon* (April 1946).

Peplau, L.A. and Perlman, D. 'Perspectives on loneliness' in L.A. Peplau and D. Perlman (eds), *Loneliness: A sourcebook of current theory, research and therapy*, pp. 1–18. New York: Wiley (1982).

Pert, C. *Molecules of emotion: The science behind mind-body medicine*. New York: First Touchstone Edition (1999).

Pollan, M. 'The intelligent plan' in *New Yorker* (23 December 2013). Available from: www.newyorker.com/magazine/2013/12/23/the-intelligent-plant [accessed 11 December 2016].

Price, S. 'Think slow' BCCJacumen.com. (n.d.). Available from: www.priceglobal.com/media/documents/603778102_BCCJ%20UCB-SP.pdf [accessed 11 September 2016].

Richardson, A., King, S., Garrett, R. and Wrench, A. 'Thriving or just surviving? Exploring student strategies for a smoother transition to university. A practice report' in *The International Journal of the First Year in Higher Education*, 3 (2), 87–93 (2012).

Richter, M., Eck, J., Straube, T., Miltner, W.H.R. and Weiss, T. 'Do words hurt? Brain activation during the processing of pain-related words' in *Pain*, 148 (2), 198–205 (2010). https://doi.org/ 10.1016/j.pain.2009.08.009

Roberts, R., Golding, J., Towell, T., Reid, S., Woodford, S., Vetere, A. and Weinreb, I. 'Mental and physical health in students: The role of economic circumstances' in *British Journal of Health Psychology*, 5 (3), 289–297 (2000).

Rogers, C. *On becoming a person: A therapists' view of psychotherapy*, 2nd ed. New York: Mariner Books (1995).

Rosa, E.M. and Tudge, J. 'Urie Bronfenbrenner's theory of human development: Its evolution from ecology to bioecology' in *Journal of Family Theory & Review*, 5 (4), 243–258 (2013). https://doi.org/10.1111/jftr.12022

Rosenthal, R. and Jacobson, L. 'Pygmalion in the classroom' in *The Urban Review*, 3 (16), 16–20 (1968).

Ross, H. 'Exploring unconscious bias. Diversity best practices' (2008). Available from: www.cookross.com/docs/UnconsciousBias.pdf [accessed 11 September 2016].

Rozin, P. and Royzman, E.B. 'Negativity bias, negativity dominance, and contagion' in *Personality and Social Psychology Review*, 5 (4), 296–320 (2001).

Sax, L.J. 'Health trends among college freshmen' in *Journal of American College Health*, 45, 252–262 (1997).

Schure, M.B., Christopher, J. and Christopher, S. 'Mind-body medicine and the art of self care: Teaching mindfulness to counseling students through yoga, meditation and qigong' in *Journal of Counseling and Development*, 86, 47–56 (2008).

Seligman, M.E. and Maier, S.F. 'Failure to escape traumatic shock' in *Journal of Experimental Psychology*, 74 (1), 1–9 (1967). https://doi.org/10.1037/h0024514

Seligman, M.E.P. and Csikszentmihalyi, M. 'Positive psychology: An introduction' in *American Psychologist*, 55, 5–14. (2000).

Senge, P.M. *The fifth discipline: The art & practice of the learning organization*. New York: Doubleday/Currency (1990).

Shapiro, S.L. and Carlson, L.E. *The art and science of mindfulness: Integrating mindfulness into psychology and the helping professions*. Washington, DC: American Psychological Association (2009).

Shaw, A., Joseph, S. and Linley, P.A. 'Religion, spirituality, and posttraumatic growth: A systematic review' in *Mental Health, Religion & Culture*, 8 (1), 1–11 (2005).

Siegel, D.J. 'Mindfulness training and neural integration: Differentiation of distinct streams of awareness and the cultivation of wellbeing' in *Social Cognitive and Affective Neuroscience*, 2, 259–263 (2007a).

Siegel, D.J. *The mindful brain: Reflection and attunement in the cultivation of well-being*. New York: Norton (2007b).

Tang, Y., Ma, Y., Wang, J., Fan, Y., Feng, S., Lu, Q. and Posner, M.I. 'Short-term meditation training improves attention and self-regulation' in *PNAS: Proceedings of the National Academy of Sciences of the United States of America*, 104, 17152–17156 (2007).

Ullrich, P.M. and Lutgendorf, S.K. 'Journaling about stressful events: Effects of cognitive processing and emotional expression' in *Annals of Behavioral Medicine*, 24 (3), 244–250 (2002). https://doi.org/10.1207/S15324796ABM2403_10

Universities UK. 'Higher education in numbers' (n.d.). Available from: www.universitiesuk.ac.uk/facts-and-stats/Pages/higher-education-data.aspx [accessed 15 August 2016].

Venosa, A. 'Prejudice in the brain—How evolutionarily valuable brain processes have turned problematic' in *Medical Daily* (2015). Available from: www.medicaldaily.com/prejudice-brain-how-evolutionarily-valuable-brain-processeshave-turned-problematic-344368 [accessed 11 September 2016].

Walsh, R. and Shapiro, S.L. 'The meeting of meditative disciplines and western psychology: A mutually enriching dialogue' in *American Psychologist*, 61, 227–239 (2006).

Wang, S.J. 'Mindfulness meditation: Its personal and professional impact on psychotherapists' in *Dissertation Abstracts International: Section B: Science and Engineering*, 67, 4122 (2007).

Warburton, D.E.R., Nicol, C.W. and Bredin, S.S.D. 'Health benefits of physical activity: The evidence' in *CMAJ: Canadian Medical Association Journal*, 174 (6), 801–809 (2006).

Waterman, A.S. 'Two conceptions of happiness: Contrasts of personal expressiveness (eudaimonia) and hedonic enjoyment' in *Journal of Personality and Social Psychology*, 64 (4), 678–691. (1993). https://doi.org/10.1037/0022-3514.64.4.678

Waugh, C.E., Wager, T.D., Fredrickson, B.L., Noll, D.C. and Taylor, S.F. 'The neural correlates of trait resilience when anticipating and recovering from threat' in *Social Cognitive and Affective Neuroscience*, 3, 322–332 (2008).

Werner, E.E. and Smith R.S. *Overcoming the odds: High risk children from birth to adulthood*. Ithaca, NY: Cornell University Press (1992).

Wilkie, D. 'Rooting out hidden bias' in *SHRM* (2014) Available from: www.shrm.org/publications/hrmagazine/editorialcontent/2014/1214/pages/1214-hidden-bias.aspx [accessed 11 September 2016].

Williams, J.M.G. 'Mindfulness and psychological process' in *Emotion*, 10, 1–7 (2010).

Wood, D.J., Bruner, J.S. and Ross, G. 'The role of tutoring in problem solving' in *Journal of Child Psychiatry and Psychology*, 17 (2), 89–100 (1976).

World Health Organization (WHO) *The ICD-10 classification of mental and behavioural disorders—diagnostic criteria for research*. Geneva: World Health Organization (1993).

World Health Organization (WHO) 'Skills for health. Skills-based health education including life skills: An important component of a child-friendly/health-promoting school' (2003) Available from: www.who.int/school_youth_health/media/en/sch_skills4health_03.pdf [accessed 16 May 2016].

World Health Organization (WHO) *Promoting mental health: Concepts, emerging evidence, practice (Summary Report)*. Geneva: World Health Organization (2004).

World Health Organization (WHO) *Promoting mental health: Concepts, emerging evidence, practice*. Geneva: World Health Organization (2005).

World Health Organization (WHO) 'ICD-11 beta draft' (2014). Available from: https://apps.who.int/classifications/icd11/browse/l-m/en [accessed 21 January 2016].

Wrzesniewski, A. 'Engage in job crafting' in J. Dutton and G. Spreitzer (eds) *How to be a positive leader: Insights from leading thinkers on positive organisations*. San Francisco, CA: Berrett-Koehler Publishers (2014).

Zeller, W. J. and Mosier, R. (1993). 'Culture shock and the first-year experience' in *Journal of College and University Student Housing*, 23 (2), 19–23.

Zubin, J. and Spring, B. 'Vulnerability: A new view of schizophrenia' in *Journal of Abnormal Psychology*, 86, 103–126 (1977).

Endnotes

[1] https://flourishingeducation.co.uk/podcasts/ [accessed 1 September 2021].

[2] www.theguardian.com/education/series/mental-health-a-university-crisis [accessed 21 August 2016].

[3] www.hesa.ac.uk/data-and-analysis/students/whos-in-he [accessed 15 September 2021]

[4] www.mentalhealth.org.uk/publications/fundamental-facts-about-mental-health-2016 [accessed 15 September 2021]

[5] www.thelancet.com/journals/lanpsy/article/PIIS2215-0366(20)30308-4/fulltext [accessed 15 September 2021]

[6] www.ons.gov.uk/peoplepopulationandcommunity/healthandsocialcare/healthandwellbeing/bulletins/coronavirusandhighereducationstudents/england20novemberto25november2020 [accessed 15 September 2021]

[7] YoungMinds Coronavirus: impact on young people with mental health needs. (2020). https://youngminds.org.uk/media/3708/coronavirus-report_march2020.pdf [accessed 15 September 2021]

[8] www.aviva.co.uk/library/pdfs/health/hotn-spring-2012-gen4421.pdf [accessed 01 October 2021]

[9] www.nus.org.uk/articles/over-half-of-students-mental-health-is-worse-than-before-the-pandemic [accessed 1 October 2021]

[10] Kessler, R.C., Berglund, P., Demler, O., Jin, R., Merjkangas, K.R. and Walters, E.E. 'Lifetime prevalence and age of onset distribution of DSM IV disorders in the National Comorbidity Survey replication' in *Archives of General Psychiatry* 62 (6), 593–602 (2005).

[11] www.saltwire.com/halifax/opinion/local-perspectives/dr-stan-kutcher-we-know-how-best-to-tackle-youth-mental-health-so-lets-do-it-361629/ [accessed 21 September 2021]

[12] https://anchor.fm/flourishingeducation/episodes/Episode-4--Flourishing-and-Languishing-with-Professor-Corey-Keyes-eb9ln3

[13] www.nature.com/articles/d41586-021-02582-8 [accessed 13 September 2021]

[14] www.nusconnect.org.uk/resources/nus-silently-stressed-a-survey-into-student-mental-well-being-2011 [accessed 13 September 2021]

[15] https://www.refuge.org.uk/25-increase-in-calls-to-national-domestic-abuse-helpline-since-lockdown-measures-began/ [accessed 21 January 2022]

[16] www.theguardian.com/lifeandstyle/2020/aug/28/fear-of-failure-giving-uk-children-lowest-happiness-levels-in-europe [accessed 21 September 2021]

[17] www.oed.com/oed2/00282689; jsessionid=6C04BC77AD21CC7D7034E3096CDC0AD4 [accessed 21 September 2021]

[18] www.simplypsychology.org/operant-conditioning.htmhttps://www.simplypsychology.org/operant-conditioning.html [accessed 3 October 2021]

19 http://educationalroleoflanguage.org/erl-journal/erl-journal-issues/volume-3/2020v01p03/ [accessed 13 September 2021]

20 https://www.qaa.ac.uk/membership/collaborative-enhancement-projects/current-collaborative-enhancement-projects/embedding-mental-wellbeing [accessed 21 January 2022]

21 https://youtu.be/ivLEAlhBHPM [accessed 13 September 2021]

22 www.besselvanderkolk.com/ [accessed 13 September 2021]

23 www.ted.com/talks/kelly_mcgonigal_how_to_make_stress_your_friend.html [accessed 13 September 2021]

24 https://theraoinstitute.com/about/ [accessed 13 September 2021]

25 www.sciencedirect.com/science/article/abs/pii/S0262407919319748 [accessed 13 September 2021]

26 www.ncbi.nlm.nih.gov/pmc/articles/PMC6438088/ [accessed 4 October 2021]

27 www.youtube.com/watch?v=ELpfYCZa87g [accessed 4 October 2021]

28 www.youtube.com/watch?v=bFCOm1P_cQQ [accessed 4 October 2021]

29 https://youtu.be/-MMLea-_ifw [accessed 4 October 2021]

30 www.thresholdglobalworks.com/pdfs/nervous-system-and-resilience.pdf [accessed 4 October 2021]

31 www.newyorker.com/magazine/2013/12/23/the-intelligent-plant [4 October 2021]

32 www.jsnlp.co.uk/ [accessed 10 October 2021]

[33] www.nytimes.com/2018/10/25/style/journaling-benefits.html [accessed 4 October 2021]

[34] www.youtube.com/watch?v=IGQmdoK_ZfY&feature=youtu. be [accessed 4 October 2021]

[35] http://science.sciencemag.org/content/330/6006/932 [accessed 24 October 2021]

[36] www.ncbi.nlm.nih.gov/pmc/articles/PMC6438088/ [accessed 24 October 2021]

[37] www.ucl.ac.uk/news/2021/feb/analysis-we-asked-70000-people-how-coronavirus-affected-them [accessed 21 September 2021]

[38] www.youtube.com/watch?v=9KmH7roj-dg [accessed 24 October 2021]

[39] https://youtu.be/0gks6ceq4eQ [accessed 24 October 2021]

[40] www.mindspace.org.uk/ [accessed 24 October 2021]

[41] https://assets.publishing.service.gov.uk/government/uploads/system/uploads/attachment_data/file/832868/uk-chief-medical-officers-physical-activity-guidelines.pdf [accessed 15 December 2021]

[42] https://hubermanlab.com/master-your-sleep-and-be-more-alert-when-awake/ [accessed 24 October 2021]

[43] www.amazon.co.uk/Build-Your-Cultural-Agility-Professionals/dp/1789666619 [accessed 24 October 2021]

[44] https://onlinelibrary.wiley.com/doi/abs/10.1002/job.4030110406 [accessed 24 October 2021]

⁴⁵ www.apa.org/helpcenter/road-resilience.aspx [accessed 24 September 2021]

⁴⁶ www.nature.com/articles/s41593-017-0044-6 [accessed 22 September 2021]

⁴⁷ https://self-compassion.org/ [accessed 22 October 2021]

⁴⁸ www.goodreads.com/book/show/16243338-the-five-levels-of-attachment [accessed 4 October 2021]

⁴⁹ www.sahtouris.com [accessed 22 October 2021]

⁵⁰ https://youtu.be/RqCz-baNdEY [accessed 22 October 2021]

⁵¹ www.spiritualityhealth.com/articles/2012/01/28/cooperative-evolution-why-human-species-will-finally-grow [accessed 22 October 2021]

⁵² https://medium.com/@NataliMorad/how-to-be-an-adult-kegans-theory-of-adult-development-d63f4311b553 [accessed 24 October 2021]

⁵³ www.youtube.com/watch?v=bhRNMj6UNYY [accessed 24 October 2021]

⁵⁴ www.goodreads.com/book/show/8715809-composing-a-further-life [accessed 24 October 2021]

⁵⁵ www.youtube.com/watch?v=eXdzKBWDraM [accessed 24 October 2021]

⁵⁶ www.businessinnovationfactory.com/people/saul-kaplan/ [accessed 24 October 2021]

⁵⁷ https://higherlogicdownload.s3.amazonaws.com/ASTC/00e37246-8bd9-481f-900c-ad9d6b6b3393/UploadedImages/Ladder_of_Participation_1.pdf [accessed 25 October 2021]

58 https://strategicdoing.net/2021/09/06/strategic-doing-and-the-iceberg-model/ [accessed 24 October 2021]

59 https://strategicdoing.net/intro/ [accessed 24 October 2021]

60 www.studentminds.org.uk/charter.html [accessed 24 October 2021]

61 www.studentminds.org.uk/uploads/3/7/8/4/3784584/191208_umhc_artwork.pdf [accessed 24 October 2021]

62 www.louisewiles.com/ [accessed 25 October 2021]

63 www.michellemcquaid.com/the-change-lab/changelab/ [accessed 25 October 2021]

64 https://permahsurvey.com/ [accessed 25 October 2021]

65 https://permahsurvey.com/ [accessed 25 October 2021]

66 www.psychologytoday.com/gb/blog/suffer-the-children/201605/what-is-good-enough-mother [accessed 25 October 2021]

67 https://permahsurvey.com [accessed 25 October 2021]

68 www.davidcooperrider.com/ai-process/ [accessed 24 October 2021]

69 www.michellemcquaid.com/product/change-blueprint-book/ [accessed 24 October 2021]

70 https://peplab.web.unc.edu/wp-content/uploads/sites/18901/2019/06/FredricksonJoiner2019PPSupwardspirals.pdf [accessed 24 October2021]

71 https://bookshop.org/books/your-change-blueprint-how-to-design-deliver-an-ai-summit/9780987271488 [accessed 24 October 2021]

[72] www.ippanetwork.org/2015/12/03/introducing-workplace-wellbeing-to-organizations-the-me-we-us-model/ [accessed 25 October 2021]

[73] www.linkedin.com/in/fabienne-vailes-3601a66/ [accessed 25 October 2021]

[74] https://twitter.com/FlourishingHE [accessed 25 October 2021]

[75] www.facebook.com/groups/440260807370186 [accessed 25 October 2021]

Index